WITCHES AND WITCH-HUNTERS

WITCHES AND WITCH-HUNTERS

A reprint of

A Treatise of Witchcraft
by Alexander Roberts (1616)

The Discovery of Witches
by Mathew Hopkins (1647)

Scottish Witchcraft Trials
by J. W. Brodie (1891)

With a foreword
by
A. E. Green
Institute of Dialect and
Folk Life Studies, Leeds University

Published S. R. Publishers Ltd., 1971

Bibliographic Note

Here reproduced are three Witchcraft tracts published for the first time within a single volume and whose individual pagination has been retained.

ISBN 0 85409 696 5

Please address all enquiries to
S. R. Publishers Ltd. (address above)

Reprinted by Scolar Press Ltd.,
Menston, Yorkshire, U.K.

Foreword

These three texts are concerned with an unpleasant but fascinating episode in European history; the great witch-hunts of the late medieval and early modern period, which began in southern Europe in the fifteenth century, and spread gradually northwards (and westwards across the Atlantic) until they finally petered out around the beginning of the eighteenth century.

These savage persecutions are important because they show how a popular belief can evolve into a coherent and systematic ideology, shared by princes, bishops and peasants alike.

This extraordinary process bears comparison with any number of examples of popular hysteria, such as the perennial British fear of the Popish Plot, National Socialism's anti-semitism, and the "Red scare" in post-war U.S.A. It is often associated with periods of religious and political upheaval, of economic difficulty and social tension, when a powerful but insecure majority will tend to sublimate through violence against a minority its feelings of discontent and anxiety. Thus, we can trace the beginning of what Professor Trevor-Roper has called the "European witch-craze"[1] to orthodox Roman Catholic persecution of the heretical Albigensians and Vaudois of the twelfth century. Thereafter, witch-hunting was sporadic and localised until the fifteenth century, when it received a tremendous boost from Pope Innocent VIII's *Summis Desiderantes Affectibus* (the so-called "Witch Bull") released in 1484, and from the classic text of demonology, the *Malleus Maleficarum,* published in 1486 by the Dominican Friars Heinrich Krämer and Jakob Sprenger.

From then on, evangelical catholics and protestants alike vied with each other in the zeal of their persecutions, and in the composition of supplements to the *Malleus* in the form of sermons and printed tracts. Luther, himself a renegade Dominican, quoted the *Malleus* from the pulpit; Jean Bodin, one of the greatest intellectual figures of sixteenth century Europe, applied his incisive mind and wide learning to demanding death not only for witches but for those who did not believe in them, in his *De la Demonomanie des Sorciers.* The Jesuit Martin del Rio, a multi-lingual classical scholar, explicitly equated witch-craft with Calvinism; while John Knox in retaliation neatly juxtaposed "the

1 Hugh Trevor-Roper, *The European Witch-Craze of the 16th and 17th Centuries,* 2nd edn., Harmondsworth (Penguin Books), 1969.

Devil, the Mass and Witches". In England James I, one of the most learned of English monarchs, wrote his celebrated *Demonologie,* simultaneously correcting the "defect" which he found in Elizabeth I's statute which distinguished legally between good and bad witches. All agreed that Europe was as alive with witches as – to use an image of one of the early polemicists – an ant-heap with ants; that they threatened great spiritual, physical and social danger; and that, good and bad alike, they had to be extirpated.

Catholic and protestant agreed so well that a dissertation, on the equivalence of sorcery and heresy, delivered at the University of Louvain in 1594, by the English catholic Thomas Stapleton, was revised for delivery at a Lutheran university during the 1620s. In his *Bibliotheca Acta et Scripta Magica* (1739), Eberhard Hauber, a progressive Lutheran pastor, notes that he had a copy of Stapleton's paper, revised. The editor had deleted "Luther" and "Lutherans" and substituted "the Pope" and "Jesuits"; otherwise no change had been made, even in the original author's malediction of the Calvinists.[1]

Thus catholic and protestant writers and preachers drew on each other for details of the witch's compact with the Devil, her[2] mark, and her familiars; for descriptions of sabbats involving sexual promiscuity and unnatural foods, and of strange journeys by broom-stick or sieve; and for advice on the identification and treatment of witches.

Sceptics, of course, there were, but they were too few and unimportant to present serious opposition to the witch-hunters. The intellectual heavyweights, such as Bodin, were in the main supporters of the orthodox demonology. Others, like Bacon, Grotius, Montaigne and Descartes largely ignored the problem, in spite of its great contemporary interest. No doubt this was, in part, a matter of caution; Bacon, for instance, was Lord Chancellor under a king whose orthodoxy had found expression in an influential tract and some harsh legislation. But opportunism and self-protection are not sufficient explanations. The fundamental solution lies in the fact that these great intellects were working towards a modification of the whole cosmology upon which orthodox demonology rested.

1 Trevor-Roper, *op. cit.,* p. 139.

2 Witches were not, of course, always female; but most were.

Their work helped to dispose of that demonology by a radical modification of the intellectual context in which it existed, rather than by a direct attack on the specific issue. Of course, this did not help the poor wretches who went to the stake or the gallows (almost always after a brutal interrogation involving at least the prolonged deprivation of sleep or the traumatic ordeal of being thrown, bound head and foot, into a river, and at worst severe tortures[1]) while the philosophers indulged themselves in the luxury of thought. In the end it was the new philosophy, together with more stable social and economic conditions in Europe, which put an end to witch-hunts.

Before this happened, those who went in fear of accusation had for their defence only a handful of humanitarians without the influence to do any real good, and who were themselves at risk of persecution for their views. Johann Weyer, physician to the Duke of Cleves, argues in his *De Praestigiis Daemonum* (1563) that the supposed activities of witches were illusions; his work was denounced by Calvinists, Lutherans and catholics alike. Weyer wrote a sequel in 1577 whose chief effect was to stimulate Bodin into a crushing rebuttal in which Weyer was accused of being himself an accomplice of the Devil. Ultimately, Weyer lost his job.

The Kentish gentleman, Reginald Scot, fared little better. His *Discovery of Witches* (1584) was refuted by James I, then King of Scotland, who, when he came to the English throne, had the book burnt at Tyburn. Essentially neither Weyer nor Scot, nor those who followed them in denouncing witch-hunts, were radical enough to present a real challenge to orthodoxy. They believed in the reality of witchcraft and the diabolical pact; their arguments centred on the erroneous identification of "malancholic" and deluded persons – especially lonely old women – as witches, and on the methods by which confessions were obtained. Even such mild criticisms as these, however, were met with a storm of indignation and denunciation by the orthodox pamphleteers; and it was not until an entirely new ideological climate came to Europe that more humane – if not necessarily more rational – opinions prevailed.

1 The use of torture, though present in Scotland, was not permitted by English law, which did, however, allow the "brainwashing" techniques of deprivation of sleep, and the swimming of witches.

Historically, then, it can be seen that the witch-hunts in Europe coincided with a period of religious and political upheaval and provided a focus for social tensions. But the persecutions were not imposed on unwilling peoples by political and spiritual leaders who should have known better. Witchcraft has a sociological as well as an historical dimension; and what the demonologists did was to elaborate and codify beliefs which already existed among the mass of people. Thereafter the law provided countermeasures against bewitchment to people who had previously, it must be assumed, relied upon such informal and traditional things as the witch-bottle and the witch-post. The witch-hunts were promoted and led by educated men, but the accusation of any given witch came, as often as not, from the ordinary villager without any formal education at all; and the process which led up to an accusation began in the everyday life of the contemporary village community.

Persons accused of witchcraft in England were usually, though not always, old, female and poorer than their neighbours. The events which led up to an accusation were typically as follows: the old woman would quarrel with a neighbour, sometimes apparently arbitrarily, sometimes because she was refused the gift or loan of some small necessary such as flour or yeast; she would begin to "curse and ban", often wishing some misfortune to befall the one who had refused her. Subsequently the latter would fall sick – loss of weight or mobility, general debility or mental distraction being frequent symptoms – or some accident would befall a member of his family, or his livestock or produce would be blighted, or his butter would not come; bewitchment would be suspected, whereupon the recent quarrel would be invoked and an accusation made.

The borrowing and lending of small quantities of basic foodstuffs is, as everyone knows, a normal part of neighbourly behaviour in many, if not all, types of community. "Just popping round for a cup of sugar", then staying to gossip for a while, is a well-recognized form of social intercourse in modern English working-class communities, though those who over-indulge in the practice are disapproved of, even though they are not usually rebuffed. And it is likely that this form of social intercourse combined with mutual aid was even more prevalent in the old pre-industrial village community.

To refuse such a loan was to commit a breach of the code of neighbourly behaviour which held together, economically as well as socially, the integrated village community. But how "integrated" was the English village during the period of the witchcraft trials of the late sixteenth and seventeenth centuries?

This was a period of industrial expansion so rapid that it has been styled "an early industrial revolution."[1] This expansion, with its division of labour, would tend to produce a more heterogeneous community. Further, the sectarian difficulties discussed above would certainly have attacked the stability of the integrated community.

These facts have led one writer[2] to propose that the rise of witchcraft trials in England was due to a major change in social organisation from the "face to face" community in which all were mutually dependent and responsible and shared the same tasks and beliefs, to the fragmented modern community of individual families with diverse beliefs and interests. According to this view, the witchcraft accusations were made by the "radical" individualists against the "conservative" communalists, because the latter reminded them disquietingly of moral and social obligations which they were trying to unlearn. This theory is not proven, but it is at least the best attempt so far to discuss English witchcraft trials of the early modern period in the context of the life and aspirations of ordinary people.

We should not underestimate the importance of the fact that those accused of witchcraft often seem to have been sharp-tongued and shrewish. Obviously, such people were most likely to clash with their neighbours. More important, whereas a curse in England now usually takes the form of a banal (if fervent) obscenity[3], and is regarded by its object as no more than a serious personal insult, in the sixteenth and seventeenth centuries it was commonly both more elaborate and more explicit, and considered as a dangerous threat to personal safety.

1 J. U. Nef, *The Rise of the British Coal Industry,* 2 vols., London (Geo. Routledge), 1932, pt II, Ch. II, passim.

2 Alan Macfarlane, *Witchcraft in Tudor and Stuart England,* London (RKP) 1970, passim.

3 We still have vestigial curses such as "Drop dead", "Go to Hell", and "I hope it chokes you"; but these are probably used more in jest than earnest, and are not thought to be effective. Further, if a man is really angry and means his words to be taken seriously, he is much more likely to employ an obscenity than one of these vestigial explicit curses.

Alexander Roberts (author of the first text) records of the witch Mary Smith that after her son had been struck by a sailor named Orkton she "came foorth into the streete, cursing and banning him therefore . . . and wished in a most earnest and bitter manner, that his fingers might rot off" – which, it seems, after a sickness lasting nine months, they did, along with his toes.

However sceptical we may be of the grotesque fantasies of night-flying, sabbats, sexual intercourse with the devil, and the appearance of monstrous familiars such as Hopkins describes, there is no reason for us to suspect the testimony of those who claimed to have been physically afflicted: there seems no doubt that they genuinely did become ill, and thought that they had been bewitched. Psychogenic complaints are well known to modern medicine, and ethnological writings are full of references to death occurring in tribal societies because a person believes himself to have been bewitched. An attempt has even been made to demonstrate the physiological mechanisms by which this may occur.[1] Medical study of the records of illness supposedly caused by witchcraft in sixteenth and seventeenth century England might well discover a characteristic "bewitchment-syndrome", with symptoms which modern medicine might normally associate with psychogenic illness.

The misfortunes which occurred, allegedly as a consequence of witchcraft, were not particularly unusual. A child falling while climbing a tree; a cow giving bloody milk; butter refusing to churn – these are things which might happen in the normal course of events. Malevolent influence was so readily blamed that witchcraft beliefs in early modern Europe must have been more systematic, in the sense of being principles by which people lived, than Professor Trevor-Roper would have us believe when he rather quaintly writes them off as "elementary village credulities"[2]. The pressure behind the "witch-craze" arose out of social relationships and religious beliefs at all levels of society. Ordinary people's witchcraft beliefs did not die when the educated establishment abandoned its demonology and its witch-hunts. Francis Grose, a child of the Enlightenment, writing in

1 Walter B. Cannon, "Voodoo Death", *American Anthropologist,* XLIV (1942), pp. 169-181.

2 *op. cit.,* p. 9.

1787, might well ridicule and decry the belief and process by which some "poor, decrepit, superannuated, old woman . . . in great distress"[1] was brought to her death; but, writing over a century later about traditional beliefs in the Cleveland Hills, J. C. Atkinson could make reference to "the omnipresence of the witch and the persistency of witch-tales or legends" and comment that it would be "difficult to exaggerate the dimensions of that element of folklore."[2]

Regional folklore collections of the nineteenth and twentieth centuries indicate that notions which intellectuals had been laughing to scorn, and legislators busily removing from the statute books for a century or more, were still firmly entrenched in the minds and lives of many country-dwellers. Records of such beliefs in the great urban centres may well be absent because collectors of folk-lore have not commonly, until recently, concerned themselves with such places.

To demonstrate the intensity of such beliefs, it may be worthwhile to quote one of the great American collectors of this century:

> "A solid citizen of Little Rock, Arkansas, contends that every good Christian must believe in witchcraft. 'It's just like John Wesley said,' he told me, 'If you give up witches you might as well throw away your Bible.' "[3]

The man was showing a Biblical fundamentalism which would not have been out of place in the seventeenth century, and which would have met with the approval of Alexander Roberts.

When he published his *Treatise of Witchcraft* in 1616, Roberts was the incumbent of the parish of King's Lynn. The previous year the town had seen an outbreak of bewitchments which were attributed to one Mary Smith, the wife of a glove-maker. Mary was accused by a number of her neighbours, plus – rather unusually – a London fishmonger to whom her husband owed

1 Francis Grose, *A Provincial Glossary,* London (S. Hooper), 1787, "Superstitions" p. 17 ff.

2 Rev. J. C. Atkinson, *Forty Years in a Moorland Parish,* London (Macmillan), 1892, p. 74.

3 Vance Randolph, *Ozark Superstitions,* New York (Dover), 1964, p. 264. (First edition Columbia U.P., 1947).

money. She was interrogated, Roberts himself being present, confessed to having made a pact with the Devil, and died for her crimes on January 16th, 1616. Roberts' treatise was commissioned by the mayor and councillors of the town, perhaps in justification of their proceedings.

The *Treatise* is a learned piece of work which falls into two parts. The first is concerned with the theology of witchcraft, the second with an account of Mary's "wicked practises" against her victims. In its theological aspect, Roberts' work is as much concerned with the wiles of the Devil as with witchcraft in particular, which is seen as only one of the many "deceits" by which Satan attempts to "deprive man of that happy and blessed estate which he lost by pride, and draw him into the society of his owne damnation."

The author speaks, as he must have done often from his pulpit, of the need to be "carefull Centinels over our selves" and to resist the blandishments of "our grand adversary". Witchcraft, in fact, is seen as a manifestation of the Devil's power, and Roberts is careful to point out that to deny the existence of witches, as he claims some have done, may well be heresy. In a series of propositions, Roberts confirms the existence of witches, discusses their nature, and deals with some objections to the possibility of the diabolical pact; in all this leaning heavily on the *argumentum ad exemplum,* with material drawn from the Fathers, classical authors, and most of all from the Bible. His fundamentalism is evident throughout in his misogyny, his militant protestantism, and above all in his contention that there is no distinction to be made between good and bad witches: all deserve the extreme penalty, whether they have done harm or not, because their crime is not civil but religious, not causing milk to sour but making a pact with the Devil.

It is debatable whether his flock agreed with him. The "true narration" of Mary Smith's witchcraft, which is more or less objective reportage, shows that, while their chiliastic parson may have been warning them off from any meddling with magic (even to find lost goods or to apprehend a thief), the ordinary parishioners were worried about the damage they thought Mary was doing, rather than about her or their immortal souls. They were quite prepared to resort to magic themselves to counter Mary's arts. The father of one of her victims, Elizabeth Hancock, "had beene to aske counsell" (presumably of one of the mysterious and influential "cunning folk" who figure in contemporary accounts) and "made a Witch Cake". Thus we can see that the interests of the demonologists were not identical to those of the man in the street.

In fact, to most modern readers, Roberts' account of the actions of Mary Smith and her presumed victims will probably be of more interest than his theological propositions.

The account vividly evokes the intimate, inward-looking world of the small town and village in the early seventeenth century, and the gossip and quarrels to which the social relationships of that world gave rise. Mary's trade in cheese is undercut by a neighbour's cheap purchase of the Dutch product; thereafter he is "afflicted" every time he handles cheese. Cicely Balye, servant to Mary's next-door neighbour, spies on her through the party-wall, and sees her kneeling and "uttering many murmuring, broken and imperfect speeches" – which Cicely interprets as diabolical rites, though a more rational explanation might be that she was merely praying. Mary calls the buxom servant-girl a "great fat-tailed sow", and threatens that she will waste away, which she does. Mary's cat frequents the house of Elizabeth Hancock's second husband, James Scot, who, with some difficulty, kills it. Later, Mary threatens Elizabeth with a broom and defiles her clothes, and when James threatens her with prosecution "she clapped her hands, and said hee killed her cat". The exchanges between Mary and her neighbours are penned with dramatic clarity, and the reader is made to feel most strongly the strange atmosphere in which a man could become so afraid of a woman known to him personally that when he attempted to scratch her (a traditional remedy against witchcraft) "his nailes turned like feathers, having no strength to lay his hands upon her."

The Discovery of Witches, by the notorious Matthew Hopkins, self-styled Witch Finder General, contains no such dramatic account of accusations of witchcraft. It is a much briefer and altogether more personal document than Roberts' treatise.

Hopkins was the son of a Suffolk minister, and by profession a lawyer, practising first at Ipswich and thereafter at Manningtree, also in Essex.[1] It was there, in March 1644, that he accidentally discovered, as he tells us, the "sect" of witches with which his detective career began. The trial of this group of witches took place in July 1645; as a result of it, something approaching thirty people were condemned to death, and evidence emerged which suggested that witches were also operating in the neighbouring county of Suffolk. What had started by accident was continued by design. Hopkins extended his investigations into Suffolk, and then – as cross-accusations between accused witches multiplied under the stimulus of Hopkins' interrogations and the fame of the witch-finder spread – into Norfolk, Huntingdonshire, and Cambridgeshire.

He was accompanied on most of his journeys by the Calvinist lawyer John Sterne and a woman called Phillips whose responsibility it seems to have been to search the bodies of the accused for witch's marks (spots insensible to pain) and supernumerary teats by which they were supposed to suckle their familiars. The three were paid for their services, and no doubt this was an important part of their motivation but it would be naive to suppose that the East Anglian prosecutions of 1645 and 1646 were caused by a trio of confidence-tricksters. First, there is no reason to doubt the sincerity of their belief in witchcraft; second, although the 1645 trial showed a number of features new to English witchcraft prosecutions[2], there had been previous witch-hunts without the presence of witch-finders; finally, despite the presence of an articulate opposition to their proceedings, Hopkins and Sterne were successful. The only possible conclusion to be drawn is that they were not creating accusations of witchcraft but merely giving official sanction to suspicions which already existed.

The local opposition to Hopkins and Sterne is of some interest, both in itself and because one of its results was Hopkins'

1 Rev. Montague Summers, "The Discovery of Witches: A Study of Master Matthew Hopkins," Foreword to the Reprint of *The Discovery of Witches*, London (The Cayme Press), 1928.

2 Not the least was the very presence of witch-finders. In addition we might point to new methods of interrogation such as swimming and deprivation of sleep; the execution of an abnormally high proportion of the accused; an exceptionally high number of indictments merely for entertaining familiars; and evidence relating to the sabbat and to sexual intercourse with the Devil.

own tract. Sterne comments quite extensively on it, reporting that he, along with forty others, was outlawed on a writ of conspiracy, as a result of the influence of an important Colchester business man; he also mentions that the same man, along with another citizen of some standing, was responsible for partially thwarting their investigations in Colchester and for securing the reprieve of a witch condemned at Assize.[1] In addition, Hopkins' activities in Huntingdonshire were partly blocked by John Gaule, vicar of Great Staughton, who in 1646 first preached a thunderous sermon against the witch-finder, then published a pamphlet denouncing his activities.[2] It is possible that this pamphlet was the document criticising Hopkins which was presented to the Norfolk judges in 1646 or 1647.[3] Whatever the document was, it spurred Hopkins into publishing his defence: and every page of the *Discovery* reads like the work of a man who is aware of an increasing public distaste for his proceedings and methods, and is anxious to disarm criticism. Hopkins had, after all, every reason to be anxious: as his first Querie tells us, there were those who believed that he himself must be a witch, and if that point of view had caught on he stood a good chance of being hoist with his own petard.

He therefore went to some pains to justify his methods, and possibly to gloss over their more unpleasant features. Thus we find him claiming that deprivation of sleep, walking of witches, and swimming were methods used only "in the infancy of this discovery" and since abandoned – though he states that witches often ask to be swum because the Devil has misled them into thinking they will be cleared, and that, "peradventure their own stubborne wills did not let them sleep, though tendered and offered to them".

Hopkins was a lawyer and knew how to cover his tracks; he also knew about invalid confessions. He defines as unacceptable any confession extracted by torture, by cajolement, or by leading

1 John Sterne, *A Confirmation and Discovery of Witchcraft,* 1648. Cited by Mcfarlane, *op. cit.,* pp. 138/9.

2 John Gaule, *Select Cases of Conscience Touching Witches and Witchcraft,* 1646. See Summers, *op. cit.,* pp. 43/4.

3 G. L. Kittredge, *Witchcraft in Old and New England,* Cambridge, Mass. (Harvard University Press), 1929; 2nd edn., New York, 1956, pp. 594/5.

questions; and any confession of improbabilities such as flying and riding broomsticks. He emphasises that he has only accepted as valid full confessions, freely given, with details which can be checked, such as an account of damage done by witchcraft. In short, the picture which he presents of himself is that of a god-fearing and reasonable man, whose skill in finding witches is such as any adept lawyer might acquire with experience, and has nothing to do with supernatural gifts.

In the end, Hopkins' anxiety was misplaced, for he died peacefully in his bed in the very year that his justification was published. Notwithstanding, the rumour soon arose that he had been swum as a witch and, having floated, had been hanged – a legend that was still current more than a century after his death.[1]

Hopkins' tract shows that his objection to witches, like that of Roberts, was chiefly theological. He rather doubts whether witches really do any damage, and suspects that they are persuaded so by the Devil: nevertheless, they deserve to die because of their Satanic pact. There, however, the resemblance between the two ends. Unlike Roberts, Hopkins gives no impression of erudition. His theology is merely that of the interested layman, and the only work he cites in his defence is King James' *Demonologie.* Where Roberts was a theoretician of witchcraft, Hopkins seems to have been a plain and practical man; bigoted, narrow-minded and partly opportunistic no doubt, inhumane no more than many of his contemporaries, and finally no more, in all probability, than the right man in the right place at the right time.

Brodie-Innes' paper on Scottish witchcraft trials is a different kind of work from the other two. The treatises of Roberts and Hopkins were written by men who were directly involved with their subject-matter, and are essentially pieces of special pleading; Innes' monograph, written three centuries later, is an attempt at objective historical scholarship. A brief but interesting survey of the major Scottish trials, it attempts to treat the evidence on its own terms. Although he is firmly a nineteenth century rationalist, Innes is intellectually flexible enough to see that it is too easy to scoff at the testimony of witches and their accusers as delusions and fantasies; and he points to the disquieting fact that

1 See Francis Grose, *op. cit.,* "Superstitions", p. 30.

> ". . . among judges and others concerned in the Scottish Witchcraft prosecutions, and in the seemingly brutal sentences which were often pronounced, we find some of the keenest philosophical intellects and the greatest minds of the time, men whose works and opinions on every other subject are quoted with respect to this day . . . Clearly the ignorance and superstition theory, though abundantly flattering to the vanity of this age, will not account for the Witchcraft Trials."

So, to explain the testimonies of night flights, strange journeys, sabbats and diabolical manifestations, he advances a primitive psychological hypothesis of the witch or sorcerer as hypnotist, with the ability to make people believe that they had indeed participated in the events to which they bore witness. Although the suggestion does not nowadays sound particularly convincing, it is at least a notable early attempt to explain rather than dismiss the evidence of the trials.

Innes is also good at placing the trials within their historical context. He stresses the importance of religious animosity in the trials of Bessie Dunlop and Effie Makcalzane, and of the political struggle between King James and Bothwell which underlay the latter trial. In addition, he sketches in the legal context of the punishments for witchcraft, reminding us that there was no special savagery in the death penalty at a time when the same sentence could be passed for theft.

The evidence of the Scottish trials is in many ways markedly different from that of the English prosecutions. First, there is a difference in the social status of the accused. The English trials tend to involve, almost exclusively, ordinary villagers, or occasionally gentlefolk of some standing locally but with no great reputation nationally. By contrast, the Scottish trials sometimes involve people of high rank such as Lady Munro of Fowlis and Effie Makcalzane, heiress of Lord Cliftonhall, and the political and religious aspects of the trials are correspondingly more marked. Second, different aspects of the supernatural appear in the Scottish evidence, most notably that of fairy-belief. The testimonies of Bessie Dunlop, the first witch to be burned in Scotland, in 1576, and of Alison Peirson, in 1588, both claim to be associate witches with the "Court of Elfhame", or Fairyland, and give accounts of the place and its inhabitants. Third, the legal process in Scotland, as on the continent, was even more ferocious than that in England, various forms of physical torture being used to extract confessions.

These three texts, then, provide a good basis for a comparison between witchcraft beliefs and trials in England and Scotland; and in addition they are illustrative of a number of sociological and psychological aspects of witch-beliefs. Finally, and perhaps most important, they have an important lesson for twentieth century man, in that they show how a combination of social insecurity and ideological complacency can easily lead otherwise decent and reasonable people into fear, hatred and ultimately persecution of their fellow-men. It may be that every society has its witch: for Germany between the wars it was the Jew; for the U.S.A. in the 'fifties it was the Communist; for the United Kingdom in the 'seventies it could yet be the coloured immigrant and his British-born children. The lesson of the witch-hunts is one we cannot afford to ignore.

A. E. GREEN
Institute of Dialect and
Folk Life Studies.

A
Treatiſe of Witchcraft.

Wherein ſundry Propoſitions are laid downe, plainely diſcouering the wickedneſſe of that damnable Art, with diuerſe other ſpeciall points annexed, not impertinent to the ſame, ſuch as ought diligently of euery Chriſtian to be conſidered.

*With a true Narration of the Witch-*crafts which ***Mary Smith***, wife of ***Henry Smith*** Glouer, did practiſe: Of her contract vocally made between the Deuill and her, in ſolemne termes, by whoſe meanes ſhe hurt ſundry perſons whom ſhe enuied: Which is confirmed by her owne confeſſion, and alſo from the publique Records of the Examination of diuerſe vpon their oathes: And *laſtly, of her death and execution, for the ſame; which was on the twelfth day of Ianua-rie laſt paſt.*

By ALEXANDER ROBERTS B. D. and Preacher of Gods Word at *Kings-Linne* in *Norffolke*.

EXOD. 22. 18.
Thou ſhalt not ſuffer a Witch to liue.

Impium eſt nos illis eſſe Remiſſos, quos cœleſtis Pietas Non Patitur impunitos: Alarus Rex apud Caſſiodorum.

LONDON,
Printed by N. O. for SAMVEL MAN, and are to be ſold at his Shop in Pauls Church-yard at the ſigne of the Ball.
1616.

¶ To the right Worshipfull Maister *Iohn Atkin Maior*, *the Recorder* and Aldermen, and to the Common Counsaile, Burgesses and Inhabitants of *Kings Linne in Norffolke*, Grace and Peace.

Right worshipfull:

IN these last dayes, and perillous times, among the rest of those dreadfull euills, which are fore-told should abound in them, a close & disguised contempt of religion may be iustly accounted as chiefe, which causeth and bringeth vpon men all disastrous effects, when although it be shadowed with a beautifull Maske of holines, faire tongued: yet false-harted,[a] *professing they know God, but in works deny him.* And among these there be two especiall sorts; the one, who entertaining a stubborne, and curious rash boldnes, striue by the iudgemēt of reason, to search ouer-deeply into the knowledge of those things which are farre aboue the reach of any humane capacitie. And so making shipwracke in this deep and vnsoundable Sea, ouerwhelme themselues in the gulfe thereof. The other kind is more sottish, dull, and of a slow wit,

2. Timoth. 3. 5.

[a] *Titus 1. 16.*

and therefore ouer-credulous, beleeuing euerie thing, especially when they be carried by the violent tempest of their desires, and other vngouerned affections; and among these the diuell vsually spreadeth his netts, as assured of a prey, wayting closely if hee can espie any, who either grow discontented and desperate, through want and pouerty, or be exasperated with a wrathfull and vnruly passion of reuenge, or transported by vnsatiable loue to obtaine some thing they desire; and these hee taking aduantage, assaulteth with golden and glorious promises, to performe vnto them the wishes of their owne hearts; the drift whereof is (hee being as at the first incased in a subtile Serpents skinne) onely to enthrall and invassall them slaues to himselfe. The first of these mentioned, are slie and masked Atheists, who ouer-shadow their secret impiety, loose and dissolute behauiour with some outward conformitie and shew of religion, snatching (as they thinke) a sufficient warrantize thereof from those disorders they obserue among men, and therfore passe vncensured, hauing a ciuill, but dissembled carriage. The second be Sorcerers, Wisards, Witches, and the rest of that ranke and kindred: no small multitude swarming now in the world, yet supposed of many, rather worthy pitty then punishment, as deluded by fantasies, and mis-led, not effecting those harmes wherewith they bee charged, or themselues acknowledge. But considering they be ioyned and linked together with Satan in a league (the common and professed e-

nemy

nemy of mankinde) and by his helpe performe many subtile mischieuous actions, and hurtfull designes, it is strange that from so great a smoake arising, they neither descrie nor feare some fire. And therefore, in respect of these, I haue at your appointment and request (for whom I am most willing to bestow my best labours and euer shall be) penned this small Treatise, occasioned by the detection of a late witch among you, whose irreligious care, and vnwearied industry, is not to be defrauded of deserued commendation, and by mature deliberation, and discreete search, found out her irreligious and impious demeanour, and also discouered sundry her vnnaturall and inhumane mischiefes done to others, whereof being conuicted, she was accordingly sentenced, and did vndergoe the penalty iustly appointed, and due by Law vnto malefactors of that kinde. After all which, you kindled with a holy zeale of the aduauncement of Gods glorie, and giuing satisfaction to euery one howsoeuer affected, intermitted no meanes, vsing therein the labour of your carefull Ministers (willingly offering themselues in this holy seruice) whereby she might be broght (as one conuerted in the last houre) to the sight & acknowledgement of her heinous sins in generall, & particularly of that of witchcraft, confessing the same, & by true repentance, and embracing of the tender mercies of God in Christ Iesus saue her soule (who refuseth no true and vnfained conuert at any time.) And hee gratiously blessing these religious endeuors of yours, vouchſafed to ſecond the ſame with a happy and wiſhed for euent, which (as I hope) ſhall appeare manifeſtly in the following Treatiſe vnto all thoſe who are not fondly, & without cauſe, too much wedded to their owne conceits: And thus, deſiring GOD moſt humbly to confirme and ſtrengthen you in his truth, which euer you haue loued, and is your due praiſe, and ſhall be at the laſt an honour vnto you: I reſt

Your Worſhips in all Chriſtian duty
to be commaunded,

A. Roberts.

To the Reader.

CHristian Reader, I haue vpon occasion penned this short discourse, and that of such a subiect wherewith not being well acquainted, am enforced to craue some direction from those, whose names you shall finde remembred in the same: (that I be not vnthankefull vnto those from whom I receiue instruction) and haue in former time, and latter dayes, taken paines in searching out, both the speculatiue, and practique parts of this damnable Art of Witchcraft, a dangerous and seducing inuention of Sathan, who from the Arcenals, and Magicians store-houses of his ancient and mischieuous furniture, hath not spared to affoord all helpe, and the best Engines for the subuerting of soules, pliable to his allurements: and to this end, beside a plaine narration of fact in this case committed and confessed, (least the Treatise should be too bare and naked) I haue added thereunto a few Propositions, agreeing to such a subiect matter, manifesting some speciall poynts not altogether impertinent in my opinion, nor vnworthy of due consideration: I know mine owne wants, and do as willingly acknowledge them: One more experienced, and of greater leasure, and better health, had beene fitter for the opening and discouering of so deepe a mystery, and hidden secret of Iniquity, as this is; and haply hereafter may be willing to take that taske in hand: yet herein thou shalt finde something not vsuall: A manifest contract made with the Diuell, and by the solemne tearmes of a league, which is the ground of all the pernitious actions proceeding from those sorts of people, who are, haue beene, and shall be practitioners in that cursed and hellish Art. And yet no more then she, that Witch of whom

in

in this relation we do ſpeake, hath of her owne accord, and voluntarily acknowledged after conference had wit hme, and ſundry learned and reuerend Diuines, who both prayed for her conuerſion, carefully inſtructed her in the way to ſaluation, and hopefully reſcued her from the Diuell, (to whom ſhe was deuoted, and by him ſeduced) and regained her to God, from whom ſhe was departed by Apoſtacie. And in this ſo Chriſtian and holy action were the continuall paines of

Maiſter { Thomas Howes.
Thomas Hares.
Iohn Man.
William Leedes.
Robert Burward.
William Armitage.

And of theſe in the day of execution (which ſhe in no wiſe would condiſcend vnto ſhould be deferred, though offered repriuall vpon hope that more might haue beene acknowledged) being very diſtemperate, neuertheleſſe ſome accompanied her to the place, and were both eye and eare-witneſſes of her behauiour there, ſeeing and hearing how ſhe did then particularly confeſſe her confederacy with the Diuell, curſing, banning, and enuy towards her neighbours, and hurts done to them, expreſſing euery one by name, ſo many as be in the following diſcourſe, nominated, and how ſhe craued mercy of God, and pardon for her offences, with other more ſpecialties afterward expreſſed. And thus I end, taking my leaue, and commending thee to the gracious guidance and preſeruation of our good God in our bleſſed Sauiour Chriſt Ieſus.

Thine euer in the Lord,

A. Roberts.

A TREATISE OF THE CONFESSION AND EXECVTION OF *MARY SMITH*, *CONVICTED OF WITCHCRAFT*, and condemned for the ſame: of her contract vocally & in ſolemne tearmes made with the Diuell; by whoſe meanes ſhe hurt ſundry perſons whom ſhe enuied, with ſome neceſſary Propoſitions added thereunto, diſcouering the wickedneſſe of that damnable Art, and diuers other ſpeciall poynts, not impertinent vnto the ſame, ſuch as ought diligently of euery Chriſtian to bee conſidered.

THERE is ſome diuerſitie of iudgement among the learned, who ſhould be the firſt Author and Inuenter of Magicall and curious Arts. The moſt generall occurrence of opinion is, that they fetch their pedigree from the [a] *Perſians*, who ſearching more deeply into the ſecrets of Nature then others, and not contented to bound themſelues within the limits thereof, fell foule of the Diuell, and were inſnared in his nets.

[a] *Auguſtinus de diuinatione Dæmonum: & de Ciuitate Dei. lib. 7. cap 35. Plinius hiſtoriæ naturalis lib. 30. cap. 1.*

And among these, the publisher vnto the world was *Zoroaster*, who so soone as he by birth [b] entred the world, contrary to the vsuall condition of other men, laughed (whereas the beginning of our life is a sob, the end a sigh) and this was ominous to himselfe, no warrantise for the enioying of the pleasures of this life, ouercome in battell by *Ninus*[c] King of the *Assyrians*, and ending his dayes by the stroake of a thunder-bolt, and could not, though a famous Sorcerer, either fore-see, or preuent his owne destinie. And because he writ many bookes of this damnable Art, and left them to posterity, may well be accounted a chiefe maister of the same. But the Diuell [d] must haue the precedencie, whose schollers both he and the rest were, who followed treading in his steps. For he taught them South-saying, Auguration, Necromancie, and the rest, meere delusions, aiming therein at no other marke, then to with draw men from the true worshipping of God. And all these pernitious practises are fast tied together by the tailes, though their faces looke sundry wayes; and therefore the Professors thereof are stiled by sundry names, as Magitians, Necromancers, Inchanters, Wisards, Hagges, Fortune-tellers, Diuiners, Witches, Cunning Men, and Women, &c. Whose Art is such a hidden mystery of [e] wickednesse, and so vnsearchable a depth of Sathan, that neither the secrets of the one can be discouered, nor the bottome of the other further sounded,

[b] *Augustinus de Ciuitate Dei. lib. 21. cap. 14.*

[c] *Iustinus in Epitome Trogi Pompey. lib 1.*

[d] *Lactantius de origine erroris. lib. 2. cap. 17.* And citeth the testimony of *Sibilla Eritbræa* for proofe hereof. *Gratianus Decretorum part. 2. causa 26 quæst. 2. Canone sine saluatore, & inuentas esse has artes* περὶ ἀπώλειαν ἐλθεῖν ἀνθρώπων τῶν ἐκ διὰς ὑπολειπομένων εἰς ταῦτα ὑπὸ τοῦ διαβόλου. *affirmat Cedrenus in historiæ compendio.*

[e] *Probationes ex quibus legitimũ est Iudicia fieri, tres necessariæ planè dici & indubitatæ possunt 1ª veritas notorij & permanentis facti. 2ª confessio voluntaria eius qui reus factus est, atque peractus 3ª certorum testium firmorumque testimonium: his & 4ª addi potest violentæ præsumptiones de Bodinus de Dæmonomania lib. 4. cap. 2. 3. 4.*

then

then either the practisers thereof themselues by their owne voluntary confessions made, or procured by order of Iustice (according to the manner of that Countrey where they be questioned) haue acknowledged, or is manifested by the sundry mischiefes done of them vnto others, proued by impartiall testimonies vpon oath, and by vehement presumptions confirmed, or else communicated vnto vs in the learned Treatises, and discourses of ancient and late Writers gathered from the same grounds. And [f] although this Hellish Art be not now so frequent as heretofore, since the Pagans haue beene conuerted vnto Christianity, and the thick fogges of Popery ouer-mantling the bright shining beames of the Gospel of *Iesus Christ* (who came to dissolue the workes of the Diuell .1. *Ioh.* 3.8.) and were by the sincere and powerfull preaching therof dispersed; yet considering these bee the last times, dayes euill & dangerous, fore-told that should come, 2. *Tim.* 3. 1. in which iniquity must abound, *Mat.* 24. 12. and as a raging deluge ouer-runne all, so that Faith shall scarce be found vpon earth, *Luk.* 18.8. and the Diuell loosed from his thousand yeares imprisonment, * *Reuel* 20. 3. enraged with great wrath walketh about, and seeketh whom he may deuoure. 1. *Pet.* 5. 8. Because he knoweth hee hath but a short time, *Reu.* 12. 12. Before I enter into the particularity of the narra-

[f] The Oracles of the Pagans in all places of the world, whē CHRIST was borne, were silenced, and the Diuell became mute: so that *Augustus Cæsar* demanding of *Apollo* by his messengers, sent to *Delphos*, had this answer returned, παῖς ἑβραῖος κέλεται &c. in sence thus much, *An Hebrue Childe commandeth me to leaue this place, and returne againe to hell.* From hence therefore you must depart from our Altars, without resolution of any questions propounded. *Eusebius de præparatione Euangelica. lib. 5. cap 8. Theodoretus de Græcorum affectionum curatione qui est de oraculis* μετὰ τὴν τοῦ σωτῆρος ἡμῶν ἐπιφάνειαν ἀπέδρασαν οἱ τῷ δὲ τὴν ἐξαπάτην τοῖς ἀνθρώποις προσφέροντες, *Vide & Suidam in Augusto, & Athanasium de incarnatione verbi.*

* *De hac ligatione & solutione Diaboli plenissimè August. de Ciuitate Dei, lib. 20. cap. 8.*

tion intended, it ſhall be materiall to ſet downe ſome generall propoſitions, as a handfull of gleanings gathered in the plentifull harueſt of ſuch learned men, who haue written of this argument, whereby the erronious may be recalled, the weake ſtrengthened, the ignorant informed, and ſuch as iudge aright already, confirmed: and among many other theſe as chiefe, all which you ſhall ſee exemplified in the following Diſcourſe.

The firſt Propoſition.

IT is a *Quære*, though needleſſe, whether there be any Witches: for they [g] haue ſome *Proctors* who plead a nullitie in this caſe, perſwade themſelues, and would induce others to be of the ſame minde, that there be no Witches at all: but a ſort of melancholique, aged, and ignorant Women, deluded in their imagination; and acknowledge ſuch things to be effected by them, which are vnpoſſible, vnlikely, and they neuer did; and therefore Magiſtrates who inflict any puniſhment vpon them, be vnmercifull and cruell Butchers. Yet by the way, and their good leaue, who take vpon them this Apology, all who are conuented vpon theſe vnlawfull action, are not ſtrucken in yeares; but ſome euen in the flower of their youth be nuzzled vp in the ſame, and conuicted to be practiſers thereof; neither be they ouerflowed with a blacke melancholique humor, dazeling the phantaſie, but haue

[g] *Wierus de magorũ infamium pœnis lib 6. cap.* 17. 18 19 20 21 22 23 24 *&c.* 27. *& de Lamijs lib* 3. *cap* 7. *& de lamiarum impotentia.* But this poſition commeth from another as dangerous, euen Infidelity denying that there be any Diuels, but in opinion; which was the doctrine of *Ariſtotle*, and the Peripatetique Philoſophers. *Pompnatius de incantationibus Binsfeldius de confeſſionibus maleficorum*

haue their vnderſtandings cleere, and wits as quicke as other: Neither yet be they all women, though for the moſt part that ſexe be inclinable thereunto: (as ſhall afterward be ſhewed, and the cauſes thereof) but men alſo on whoſe behalfe no exception can be laid, why any ſhould demurre either of their offence or puniſhment for the ſame. Wherefore for this point, and confirmation of the affirmatiue, wee haue ſundry pregnant and euident proofes.

Firſt teſtimonies Diuine and Humane: Diuine of *God* himſelfe in his word,[h] left for our inſtruction in all dogmaticall truth, reproofe and confutation of falſhood in opinions, correction for the reforming of miſdemeaners in conuerſation, doctrine for the guidance of euery eſtate Politicall, Eccleſiaſticall, Oeconomicall. 2. *Timoth.* 3. 16. Therefore expreſſely, *Thou ſhalt not ſuffer a witch to liue, Exod.* 22. 18. [i] but to bee executed in the ſame day wherein ſhe is conuicted, and this was a cuſtome obſerued by the ancient Fathers.

[h] Διδασκαλία ἔλεγχος ἐπανόρθωσις παιδεία.

[i] *Philo in libro de legibus ſpecialibus.*

And *Deuteronomy* 18. 10. 11. there is a blacke Bill ſet downe[k], and regiſtred of ſundry kinds of theſe ſlaues of Sathan, all condemned, and God addeth in the ſame place the reaſons of this his ſeuere and ſharpe iudgement againſt them. Firſt, becauſe they are an abhomination vnto him. Secondly, he determineth vtterly to deſtroy all ſuch, and giueth his people the Iſraelites an example thereof in the Canaanites, whom their Land ſpewed out. Thirdly, for that he requireth all who belong vnto him, to be pure, vndefiled and holy,

[k] *Vide Paulum Phagium in annotationibus, & Chaldaicam Paraphraſin in cap* 18. & 19 *Leuitici.*

not ſtained with impieties,for they are bound vnto him by couenant in obedience. Fourthly,ſuch were the Heathen, ſtrangers from God, blinded in their dark vnderſtanding, without ſauing knowledge,with whom the Iſraelites, a choſen and peculiar nation,enioying his lawes and ſtatutes,muſt haue no familiarity. Further, the woman of *Endor* acknowledgeth herſelfe to be one of the rank. 1.*Sam*.28.9. And *Ieſabel*,mother of *Ieboram*, is in plaine tearmes ſtiled a Witch.2.*King*.9.22. who [l] is ſuppoſed to haue brought this Art, and the Profeſſors thereof into *Samaria*, which there continued for the ſpace of ſixe hundred yeares. Inſomuch that it was rife in common ſpeech, when any would reproach another, to doe the ſame in this forme; *Thou art a Samaritan, and haſt a Diuell* (a familiar ſpirit) which the malicious Iewes, not abiding his heauenly and gracious doctrine, obiected to Chriſt Ieſus our bleſſed Sauiour, *Ioh*. 8.48. The holy Apoſtle reprouing the *Galathians* for their ſudden Apoſtaſie and back-ſliding from the Goſpell ſo powerfully preached vnto them and with ſo great euidence of the ſpirit,as though Chriſt had bin crucified before their eyes, doth it in no other termes then theſe, *who hath bewitched you? Gal*.3.1. And afterward,*Cap*. 5. 20. marſhalleth Witch-craft among the workes of the fleſh: In both which places the names are taken from the ſeducements and illuſions of Inchanters, who aſtoniſh the mindes, and deceiue the ſenſes of men, and all that by vertue of a contract paſſed betweene them and the Diuell. Other like proofes may

[l] *Bodinus in confutatione opinionum Wieri.*

may be added to these alledged, *Leuit*. 20.6. *Micah* 5.12. *Nahum* 3.4. Now then when God affirmeth there be such, whose words are truth, shall man dare once to open his mouth, and contradict the most righteous?

Concerning humane witnesses, they be almost infinite; and therefore it shall be sufficient to produce some few, choyce, and selected: [m] The second Councell of *Constantinople* held and gathered together in the Imperiall palace, of two hundred seuen and twenty learned and reuerent Bishops, nameth sundry sorts of such Sorcerers, and censureth their actions to be the damned practises of the Pagans, and decreeth all the Agents therein excommunicated from the Church and society of Christian people, adding the motiue reason of this their determined sentence, from the Apostle, 2. *Cor*. 6. 14. For righteousnesse hath no fellowship with vnrighteousnesse, neither is there communion of light with darknesse, nor concord with Christ and Belial, nor the beleeuer can haue part with an Infidell. And [n] *Chrysostome* sharply reproueth all such, and those who aduise with them vpon any occasion, confuting the reasons which they take to be sufficient warrantise of their doings. As among the rest they will pretend, Shee was a Christian woman who doth thus charme or inchant; and taketh no other but the name of God in her mouth, vseth the words of sacred Scripture. To this that holy Father replieth,

[m] *Cap* 61. *congregata est hæc synodus sub Iustiniano qui vocatus est* ῥινοτμητης, *in qua erant Episcopi, 227. Balsamon in suis ad eum Commentariys, & vocata est synodus in Trullo erat autem ὁ* τρόυλλος *Secretarium palatij quia in eo fuit celebrata, eam autē* πενθεκτην *vocat Balsamon quasi Quintisextā dicas quia quod quinta & sexta synodis deerat (septem enim recipiunt Græci) hæc expleuit, Nomenclator Græcorum dictionum quæ apud Harmenopulum occurrunt in sui iuris Promptuario.*

[n] This testimony of *Chrysostome* is cited by *Balsamon*, in his exposition vpon that Chapter of the Councell before alleaged, to which may be added other of the same holy Bishop in his 9 *Homily* vpon the Epistle to the *Colossians*, & his 6 Sermon against the *Iewes*.

plieth, Therefore ſhe is the more to be hated, becauſe ſhee hath abuſed and taken in vaine that great and glorious name, and profeſſing herſelfe a Chriſtian, yet practiſeth the * damnable Arts of miſcreant and vnbeleeuing Heathen. For the Diuels could ſpeake the name of God, and neuertheleſſe were ſtill Diuels; and when they ſaid vnto Chriſt, they knew who he was, the holy one of God, &c. *Mar.* 1.24.25. their mouthes were ſtopped, he would no ſuch witneſſe, that wee ſhould learne, not to beleeue them when they ſay the truth: for this is but a bait, that wee might afterward follow their lies. There is much mention made of theſe, both in the Ciuill and [n] Canon Lawes, and diuerſitie of puniſhment alotted out for them; ſo that none can doubt but that there hath beene, and are ſuch. I might remember vntō you the authority of *Clemens Romanus* in his Recognitions, and thoſe Conſtitutions which āre fathered vpon the Apoſtles; but their credit is not ſo great, that they may without exception be impannelled vpon this Iury, for they haue long ſince been chalenged of [o] inſufficiencie.

Among the Gentiles, when theſe ſo qualitied perſons did ſwarme, and were accounted of high eſteeme, there be reckoned vp whole troopes of this blacke guard of the Diuell; As [p] *Circe* whom *Homer* reporteth to haue turned *Vlyſſes* Companions into Wolues, Lyons, Swine, &c. by her Inchantments, inſauaging and making them beaſt-like and furious. *Medea* [q] famous in this kinde, for ſhe murthered by Witch-craft *Glauca*

in

* *Superſtitio tãto peior eſt quãto plura miſcentur bona, quoniã vnde debeat honorari Deus honoratur Diabolus.* Ioh. Gerſon *in Trilogio Aſtrologiæ Theologiſatæ propoſitione* 21.

[n] *Vide Phothiũ Patriarchã Conſtantinopolitanũ in nono Canone titulo* 13. *cap.* 19

[o] *Ierome* in his Apology againſt *Ruffinus.* and *Euſebius* aloweth but one only Epiſtle of his, *Hiſtor. Eccleſiaſt.* 2-*cap.* 16. *Gratianus diſtinct.* 15. *Epiphanius contra Audianos.*

[p] *Homer. odiſſea* 10, φαρμάκοις ἤλλαξε *Euſtathius.*

[q] *Euripides in Medea. Ouidius Metamorph. lib.* 7. *Pindarus Pythonum Idillio* 4. *Apollonius Argonauticorum lib.* 40.

in the day of her marriage, who enioyed *Iaſon* her loue. And [r] the Mortars of theſe two, wherein they ſtamped their Magicall drugges, wer for a long time kept in a certaine mountaine, and ſhewed as ſtrange monuments to thoſe who deſired a ſight of them. For [ſ] the Diuell furniſheth ſuch with powders, oyntments, hearbes, and like receipts, whereby they procure ſickneſſe, death, health, or worke other ſupernaturall effects. Of the ſame profeſſion were [t] *Simotha*, [u] *Ericthe*, [x] *Canidia*, and infinite others beſide, whoſe damnable memory deſerueth to be buried in euerlaſting obliuion.

But becauſe the reports of theſe may ſeeme to carry ſmall credit, for that they come from Poets, who are ſtained with the note of licentious [y] faining, and ſo put off as vaine fictions; yet ſeeing they deliuer nothing herein but that which was well knowne and vſuall in thoſe times wherein they liued, they are not ſlightly, and vpon an imagined conceit, to be reiected: for they affirme no more then is manifeſt in the records of moſt approued Hiſtories, whoſe eſſence is and muſt be [z] truth, [a] as ſtraightneſſe of a rule, or elſe deſerue not that title. In which wee reade of [b] *Martiana*, [c] *Locuſta*, [d] *Martha*, [e] *Pamphilia*, [f] *Aruna*, &c. And not to inſiſt vpon particulars, there bee infinite numbers ouerflowing euen in theſe our [g] dayes,

[r] *Scholiaſtes Theocriti Idil* 2. ἐν τῷ σεληνοδίῳ ὄρει δεικνύουσι τὰς Μηδείας καὶ Κίρκης ὅλμους ἐν οἷς ἔκοπτον τὰ φάρμακα.

[ſ] *Remigius demonolatriæ lib.* 1. *cap* 2.

[t] *Theocritus in* φαρμακευτρίᾳ, *Idil*. 2.

[u] *Lucan. Pharſalibus lib.* 6.

[x] *Horatius* Ἐπῳδῶν *lib.* 5.

[y] *Pictoribus atque Poetis quidlibet audiendi ſemper fuit æqua poteſtas.*

[z] καθάπερ ἐμψύχου σώματος τῶν ὄψεων ἐξαιρεθεισῶν ἀχρειοῦται τὸ ὅλον· οὕτως ἐξ ἱστορίας ἐὰν ἄρῃς τὴν ἀλήθειαν, τὸ καταλειπόμενον αὐτῆς, ἀνωφελὲς γίγνεται διήγημα. Polib. hiſtoriarum lib. 12.

[a] *Timaus* Κάνονος ἰδιότης εὐθεῖα. [b] *Tacitus Annal. lib.* 2. [c] *Idem annal. lib.* 12. & 13 & *Suetonius in Claudio c.* 33. [d] *Plutarchus in Mario.* [e] Apuleius. [f] *Munſterus Coſmographiæ lib.* 2. [g] *Remigius*, a iudge in theſe caſes reporteth of 900 executed in Lorayne for this offence of Witch-craft in the time of his gouernement.

ſince the ſinceritie of Chriſtian Profeſſion hath decreaſed, and beene in a ſort ecclipſed in the hearts of men: for the period of the continuance thereof (after it be once imbraced) in his firſt integrity, either for zeale of affection, or ſtrictneſſe of diſcipline, hath beene by ſome learned Diuines[h] obſerued, to bee confined within the compaſſe of twenty yeares; and then afterward by degrees, the one waxed cold, and the other diſſolute: which being ſo, it is not to be marueiled though the Diuell now begin to ſhew himſelfe in theſe his inſtruments, as heretofore, though he cannot in the ſame meaſure, in reſpect of thoſe ſparkes of light which yet ſhine amongſt vs. But of this ſo much now, becauſe I ſhall haue afterward occaſion further to enlarge this poynt.

[h] *Lutherus in Geneſin.*

Againe, the policie of all States[i] haue prouided for the rooting out of theſe poyſonfull Weedes, and cutting of theſe rotten and infected members; and therefore infallibly prouing their exiſtence and being: for all[k] penall lawes looke to matters of fact, and are made to puniſh for the preſent, and preuent in future, ſome wicked actions already committed. And therefore *Solon* the Athenian making ſtatutes for the ſetling of that Common-wealth, when a defect was found, that he omitted to prouide a cautelous reſtraint, and appoint[l] anſwerable puniſhmẽt for ſuch who had killed their parents, anſwered, He neuer ſuſpected there were or would be any ſuch. Wherefore to confirme the poſition ſet downe, God doth not

[i] *Binfeldius de confeſſionibus maleficorum*, calleth this reaſon a moſt ſtrong & conuincing argument.

[k] *Ex malis moribus bonæ naſcuntur leges.*

[l] *Diogenes Laertius lib. 1. de vitis Philoſophorum in Solone.*

Cicero in Oratione pro Roſcio Amerino.

not threaten to cast away his people for murther, incest, tyranny, &c. But Sorcery, *Leuit*.20.6. And *Samuel* willing to shew *Saul* the grieuousnesse of his disobedience, compareth it to witchcraft, 1.*Sam*.15.23. The Holy Ghost also manifesting how highly God was displeased with *Manasses*, maketh this the reason, because hee gaue himselfe to Witch-craft, and to Charming, and to Sorcery, and vsed them who had familiar spirits, and did much euill in the sight of the Lord to anger him, 2.*Chro*.33.6. And for this offence were the ten tribes of Israell led into captiuitie, 2.*King*.17.17. [m] The twelue Tables of the Romans (the ancientest law they haue) by a solemne Embassage (sent for that purpose) obtained from *Athens*, & accounted as a Library of knowledge, do both make mention of such malefactors, & decree a penaltie to be inflicted vpon them. [n] *Constantius* and *Constantinus* thinke them worthy of some vnusuall death, as enemies of mankinde, strangers from nature: [o] and *Iulius Paulus* distinguishing the punishment according to the different qualitie of the offenders, pronounceth out of the then receiued opinions, that the better sort found guilty, were to dye (not determining the manner) those of meaner condition either to bee crucified, or deuoured of wilde beasts.

Our ancient Saxon Kings before the [p] Conquest, haue in their municipall Lawes apparantly demonstrated what they conceiued of these so dangerous and diuellish persons. *Alucidus* keepeth the expresse words of God: *Fæminas sagas*

[m] Of these 12. Tables *Liuie* in the 3 booke of his first Decad. *Dionysius Halicarnasseus* 10 Booke of his History, & *Iohannes Rosimus* most fully in the 6 chapter of his 8 booke of Roman antiquities. *Liuius. Plinius lib.34.cap.5. Cicero de legibus, lib.2.& de de orato primo.*

[n] *Cod.lib.9.titul.* 18.*lege multi magicis actibus.*

[o] *Sententiarum receptarum lib.* 5.*cap.* 25. *ad legem Corneliam de sicarijs & maleficis. Paulus Iurisconsultus.*

[p] *In* ἀρχαιονομια *siue de priscis Anglorum legibus Guilielmus Lambertus.*

ne sinito viuere. Suffer not women Witches to liue. *Gunthrunus* and *Canutus* will haue them, being once apprehended (that the rest of the people might bee pure and vndefiled) sent into banishment, or if they abide in the kingdome (continuing their lewd practises) executed according to desert. So *Athelstane*, if they be conuicted to haue killed any,&c. And how the present estate standeth affected toward them, the sundry strict statutes in this case prouided, may giue any, not wedded to his owne stubbornenesse, sufficient and full satisfaction. Wherefore not to erect a Tabernacle, and dwell longer in perswading an vndeniable truth, that there bee Sorcerers and Witches, I leaue these Hellish Infidels, and proceede.

The second Proposition.

q Danæus de sortiariys, cap. 20

THe second Proposition: q Who those be, and of what quality, that are thus ensnared of the Diuell, and vndermined by his fraudes. For resolution whereof, this may suffice. Those who either maliciously reiect the Gospell offered vnto them: or receiuing and vnderstanding the same, do but coldly respect, and carelesly taste it, without making any due estimation, or hauing any reuerent regard therof. In both which is a manifest and open contempt of God. For as he purposing to honour the first comming of his Sonne into

the

the World, cloathed in the cloud of our flesh, which he assumed then, suffered many to be really possessed of Diuels, to bee lunatique, deafe, dumbe, blinde, &c. whom he might deliuer from these torments, and so make apparant his glory, and shew by these his miracles wrought, that hee was the promised Messias, *Esay* 35.5.6. And therfore Christ referreth those Disciples whom *Iohn* sent vnto him (doubting in respect of that base forme which he tooke, and demanding whether it was he that should come, or another to be looked for) vnto his Doctrine and Workes; and by them to bee instructed, whereof they were then both hearers and beholders, *Math.*11.3.4.5. So now comming in the dew of his grace, and hauing restored the light of the Gospell, and bestowed that vpon mankinde, as an especiall and vnvaluable blessing, in his iustice giueth ouer the despisers thereof vnto the power of Sathan, whereby both others who contemne the same, might by their dreadfull example bee terrified, and the faithfull stirred vp to a respectiue thankfulnesse, for so great a mercy vouchsafed vnto them, and acknowledge their happinesse in being made partakers thereof, and by especiall fauour deliuered out of the tyranny of the Diuell: For this is one of the fearefull iudgements of God, and hidden from vs (as all are a great depth, *Psal.* 36. 6.) that those who receiued not the truth that they might be saued, should haue strong delusions sent vnto them, and bee giuen ouer to belieue Sathan and his lying signes, and false wonders, 2.*Thess.* 2.10.

And thus conſenting vnto ſinne, and his ſuggeſtions, they are depriued of the [r] helpe and aſſiſtance of God, and ſo diſabled to reſiſt all violent ruſhing temptations: for one offence, not being truely repented of, bringeth another, and at laſt throweth head-long downe into hell: and by this meanes man deſpiſing God his creator & redeemer, and obeying the Diuell a profeſſed enemy, and irreconciliable aduerſary, not eaſie to be confronted, becommeth his ſeruant: for of whomſoeuer any is ouercome, euen of the ſame is hee brought into bondage, 2. *Pet*. 2. 19. And the Apoſtle giueth as the reaſon why the heathen were ſo ſottiſh Idolaters, and defiled themſelues with many deteſtable and loathſome ſinnes, [s] becauſe when they knew God, they glorified him not as God, neither were thankfull, therefore God gaue them ouer to a reprobate ſence, and vile affections to doe thoſe things which were not conuenient, full of all vnrighteouſneſſe, *Rom* 1. 24. 25. &. 29 So theſe being enthralled, and deuoting themſelues to the Diuell by a mutuall league (either expreſſe or ſecret) he brandeth with his mark for his [t] owne, as in ancient time was an vſe with Bondſlaues and [u] Captiues, and theſe bee ἐζωγρημένοι, taken aliue in his ſnare, 2. *Tim*. 2. 26. and that in ſome part of the body, leaſt either ſuſpected or perceiued by vs (for hee is a cunning concealer) as vnder the eye-lids, or in the palat of the mouth,

[r] *Iaquerius in flagello Hereticorum, cap.* 18.

[s] *Peccatum ſi citius pœnitendo non tergitur, iuſto Iudicio omnipotens Deus obligatam peccantis mentem, etiam in culpam alteram permittit cadere, vt qui flendo & corrigendo noluit mundare quod fecit, peccatum incipiat peccato cumulare, Greg. Hom.* 11. *in Ezech. Auguſtinus lib.* 83. *queſtionum queſtione* 97. & *Aquinas* 1. 2. *quaeſt.* 79. *artic.* 3 & *quaeſt.* 87. *artic.* 2.

[t] *Zanchius de operibus creationis, part.* 1 *lib.* 4. *cap.* 15. *Danæus de ſortiariys cap.* 4. & *Eraſtus de Lamiys.*

[u] *De hoc more Alexander ab Alexandro. Dierum genialium lib.* 5. *cap.* 18. *Suetonius in Caligula, cap.* 27. *Cicero de officiys lib.* 2. *Cœlius Rhodinginus Antiquarum lectionum lib.* 7. *cap.* 31. & *olim militiæ Tyrones* στιγμένοι *erant & in cute ſignati Vegetius lib.* 1. *cap.* 8. & 2. *cap.* 5. *Prudentius* περὶ στεφάνων *Hymno* 10. & *huius moris meminit, Ambroſius in funebri oratione pro Valentiniano.*

or

or other ſecret places: Wherefore ſome Iudges cauſe them, once being called into queſtion, and accuſed, to be ſhauen all the body[x] ouer. And for the manner of impreſſion, or branding, it is after this ſort. The Diuell when hee hath once made the contract betweene himſelfe and the Witch, and agreed vpon the conditions, what they ſhall doe, the one for the other, giueth her ſome ſcratch[y], which remaineth ful of paine & anguiſh vntill his returne againe: at which time hee doth ſo benumme the ſame, that though it be pierced with any ſharpe inſtrument, yet is without any ſence of feeling, and will not yeeld one droppe of bloud at all: a matter knowne by iuſt, often, and due triall.

[x] *Et inſigne exemplum apud Gildemannum de Lamijs lib.* 3. *cap.* 10. *ſectione* 38.

[y] *Remigius in Dæmonolatria lib.* 1. *cap.* 5. and citeth the confeſſion of eight ſeuerall perſons, acknowledging both to haue receiued the marke and in what part of the body.

And for the moſt part, hee bringeth theſe his ſlaues and vaſſailes obliged to him as his owne, to ſome deſperate, Tragicall,[z] and diſaſtrous end; and that either by the execution of Iuſtice for their demerits, or by laying violent hands vpon themſelues, or elſe God powreth vpon them ſome ſtrange and extraordinary vengeance, or their Grand-maiſter whom they haue ſerued, diſpatcheth them in ſuch manner, as they become dreadfull and terrible ſpectacles to the beholders, whereof Hiſtories will furniſh vs with[a] varietie and plenty of examples: For the Diuell is a murthering ſpirit, deſirous to doe miſchiefe, ſwelling in pride, malitious in hatred, ſpitefull in enuy, ſubtill in craft; and therefore it behoueth euery one reſolutely to withſtand his aſſaults, *Epheſ.* 4. 27. and cautelouſly to decline his ſubtilties, and cunning

[z] *Peucerus de præcipuis diuinationum generibus titulo de Magia.*

[a] *Philippus Camerarius in Hiſtoricis medicationibus part.* 1. *cap.* 70. *&* 72.

μεθοδείας

[b] *Cyprianus in procemio libri de exhortatione ad Martyrium.*

[c] *Tatianus oratione contra Gentes.*

cunning ambushments from whence he inuadeth vs, *Eph.6.11.* [b] For this aduersary against whom we fight, is an old beaten enemy, sixe thousand yeares are fully compleat since the first time hee began to assault mankinde. But if any keepe the Commandements of God, and constantly, by a liuely faith, cleaue fast vnto Christ, he shall ouercome: for our Lord is inuincible.[c] The Diuels indeed doe willingly offer themselues to be seene of those who are not gouerned by the Holy Ghost; and that either to win themselues some estimation, or to intangle and deceiue men, vailing their treacheries vnder a smiling countenance, whom they deadly hate, for if it lay in their possibilitie, they would ouerthrow and destroy heauen it selfe. Now vnable to do this, they endeuour to worke vpon a more weake subiect and matter; and therefore hee that will not bee subdued of them, must auoid all occasions whereby he may take any aduantage, and couered with the Breast-plate of Righteousnesse, and defended with the Shield of Faith, quench all his fiery Darts. *Ephes.6.14.*

The third Proposition.

[d] *Damascenus Orthodox. fidei lib. 2. cap.4.* ἐξουσίαν ἔχει καὶ ἰσχὺν κατά τινος οἰκονομικῶς, *Iaquerius flagelli Hereticorum fascinariorum, cap. 25.*

EXcept God do by his especial grace and ouerruling power, restraine the malice of these Witches, and preserue his Children, they are permissiuely able,[d] through the helpe of the Diuell

uell their maiſter, to hurt Men and Beaſts, and trouble the elements, by vertue of that contract & agreement which they haue made with him. For man they endamage both in body & mind: In body, for [e] *Daneus* reporteth of his owne knowledge, as an eye-witneſſe thereof, that he hath ſeene the breaſts of Nurces (onely touched by their hands) thoſe ſacred fountaines of humane nouriſhment ſo dried vp that they could yeeld no milke; ſome ſuddenly tormented with extreame and intolerable paine of the Cholicke, others [f] oppreſſed with the Palſie, Leproſie, Gout, Apoplexie, &c. And thus diſabled from the performance of any action, many tortured with lingring conſumptions, [g] and not a few afflicted with ſuch diſeaſes, which neither they themſelues who wrought that euill, could afterward helpe; nor be cured thereof by the Art and diligent attendance of moſt skilfull Phyſitians. I willingly let paſſe other miſchiefes wrought by them, of which many things are deliuered in the Canon and Ciuill Lawes, in the Schoole-men, and Diuines both ancient and moderne.

In minde, ſtirring vp men to luſt, to hatred, to loue, and the like [h] paſſions, and that by altering the inward and outward ſences, either in forming ſome new obiect, or offering the ſame to the eye

[e] *Vbera matris fontes ſanctiſſimos humani generis educatores vocat Phauorinus apud A. Gellium noct. Atticarum lib.12. cap.1. Aretius problematum parte 2. Loco 144. de Magia.*

[f] *Godlemanus de veneficis lib.1 cap.7.9.21 22. 23.24 25.26. &c.*

[g] *Exempla omnem fidem ſuperantia Florentinæ mulieris & vlrici cuiuſdam Neuceſſeri refert Langius epiſt. Medicinalium lib.2. Epiſt. 38. è cuius ventriculo lignum teres & quatuor cultri execti ſunt: eorum & formam & iuſtã longitudinem ponit. Lycoſthenes lib. de prodigijs & oſtentis quo modo huiuſmodi in corporibus humanis inueniantur & qua ratione ingenerentur, aut eijciantur & an tribuenda hæc maleficijs & diabolica arti Binfeldius in commentario ad titulum Codicis de maleficis & Mathematicis pag.510.*

[h] *Gratianus in decretis, Caietanus in ſummula titulo de maleficio. Iaquerius in flagello faſcinariorum, cap.11.12. Ioh. Nider in præceptorio, præcepto 1. ca. p11. Bodinus in Dæmonomania, lib.2. cap.*

or eare, or ſtirring the humors: for there being a neere coniunction betweene the ſenſitiue and rationall faculties of the ſoule, if the one bee affected, the other (though indirectly) muſt of neceſſity be alſo moued. As for example, when they would prouoke any to loue or hatred, they propound an obiect vnder the ſhew and appearance of that which is good and beautifull, ſo that it may be deſired and embraced: or elſe by repreſentation of that which is euill & infamous, procure diſlike and deteſtation. Neither is this any ſtrange poſition, or improbable, but may bee warranted by ſufficient authority; and therefore [i] *Conſtantius* the Emperour doth expreſſely determine, all thoſe iuſtly puniſhable who ſollicite by enchantments chaſte mindes to vncleanneſſe: And Saint [k] *Ierome* attributeth vnto them this power, that they can enforce men to hate thoſe things they ſhould loue, and affect that which they ought to auoyd: and the ground hereof hath his ſtrength from the holy Scriptures: for the Diuell is able to enflame wanton[l] luſt in the heart, and therfore is named, *the Spirit of Fornication, Oſea* 4.12. and vncleane, *Math.*12.43.

There is a very remarkeable example mentioned by *Ierome*[m], of a maiden in *Gaza*, whom a yong man louing, and not obtaining, went to *Memphis* in Egypt, and at the yeares end in his returne, being there inſtructed by a Prieſt of *Aeſculapius*, and furniſhed with Magicall Coniurations, graued in a plate of braſſe, ſtrange charming words, and pictures which he buried vnder the threſhold of

[i] *Cod. lib. 9. titulo 18. Lege eſt ſcientia, hanc legem ſugillat. Weirus de præſtigijs dæmonum* lib. 3. cap. 38.
[k] *In 3. Caput prophetę Nabūni, vide & Nazianzenum in* ἀπορρήτοις, *ſiue de arcanis vel principijs non procul à fine, & eius paraphraſten Nicetam.*
[l] *Caſſianus Collat. 7. cap. 32.*
[m] *In vita Hilarionis.*

of the doore where the virgin dwelt: by which meanes ſhe fell into a fury, pulled off the attire of her head, flung about her haire, gnaſhed with her teeth, and continually called vpon the name of her louer.

The like doth [n] *Nazianzene* report of *Cyprian* before his conuerſion (though ſome thinke it [o] was not he whoſe learned and religious writings are extant, and for the profeſſion of his faith and doctrine was crowned with Martyrdome) but another of that name, toward *Iuſtina*, whom hee laſciuiouſly [p] courted, and vnlawfully luſted after. It were eaſie for me to inſtance this in many, and to adde more teſtimonies, but my intended purpoſe was, to ſet downe onely ſome few propoſitions, whereby the iudicious reader might be ſtirred vp to a deeper ſearch, and further conſideration of theſe things: for often they driue men to a madneſſe, and other ſuch deſperate paſſions, that they become murtherers of themſelues. But this alwayes muſt be kept in minde, as a granted and infallible truth, [q] That whatſoeuer the Witch doth, it receiueth his force from that ſociety which ſhe hath with the Diuell, who ſerueth her turne in effecting what ſhe purpoſeth, and ſo they worke together as [r] aſſociates.

Now concerning beaſts they doe oftentimes kill them out-right, and that in ſundry manner, or pine and waſte them by little and little, till they be conſumed.

For [ſ] the Elements, it is an agreeing conſent of all, that they can corrupt and infect them, procure

[n] *Oratione in laudē Cypriani eandem hiſtoriā refert Nicephorus Caluſtus lib.* 5. *cap.* 27.

[o] *Prudentius* περὶ στεφάνων *de paſſione Cypriani, vnus erat iuvenum doctiſ. artibus ſiniſtris, fraude pudititiā perſtringere. &c*

[p] *Ouid. lib.* 2. *de art. amand. philtra nocent animis, vimq; fauoris habent. Propertius lib.* 4. *in lanam quandam conſuluitq; ſtriges noſtro de ſanguine & in me, hippomenes fœtæ ſemina legit equæ. Vide de his Ariſtotelem de natura animaliū lib.* 6. *cap.* 22. *Pliniū* l. 8. c. 42.

[q] *Aug. de doctr. Chriſt.* l. 2. c. 22. & 23.

[r] *Iaquerius in flagello hereticorū faſcinariorū, cap.* 6. *Martinus de Arles, p.* 436.

[ſ] *Ioh. Gerſon in Trialogio Aſtrologiæ Theologiſatæ propoſ.* 16. *Palanus in Syntagmate, l.* 5. *c.* 13

tempests, to stirre vp thunder & lightning, moue violent winds, destroy the fruits of the earth: for God hath a thousand wayes to chasten disobedient man, and whole treasures full of vengeance by his Angels, Diuels, Men, Beasts. For the whole nature of things is ready to reuenge the wrong done vnto the creator.

It were but fruitlesse labour, and ill spent, to bestow long time in confirming this so manifest a truth, and not much better then set vp a candle to giue the Sunne light when it shineth brightest in mid-heauen: yet to satisfie those who doubt hereof, I will giue a small touch of an example or two.

t *Dion. Cassius Romanæ Historiæ, lib. 60. in Claudio.*

[t] *Curius Sidius* the Roman Generall in a battell against *Salebus*, Captaine of the *Moores*, in want of water, obtained such abundance of raine from Heauen by Magicall inchantments, that it not onely sufficed the thirst of his dstiressed Souldiers, but terrified the enemies in such sort, (supposing that God had sent helpe) as of their owne accord, they sought for conditions of peace, and left the field.

u *Historia de gentibus septentrionalibus, lib. 3. cap. 13. 14. 15. 16. 17. 18. 19. &c.*

The narration of *Olaus*[u] *Magnus* which he maketh of his Northerne Wisards and Witches, would seeme to be meere fictious, and altogether incredible (as of *Ericus*, who had the winde at command, to blow alwayes from that quarter to which he would set his hat. Or *Hagbert*, who could shew herselfe in any shape, higher or lower, as she pleased, at one time so great as a Giant, at another as little as a Dwarfe: by whose Diabolicall practises mighty Armies haue beene dicomfited, and sundry others, except the truth hereof were without contradiction approued: by the experience of our owne Nauigators, who trade in *Finland, Denmarke, Lapland, Ward-house, Norway*, and other Countries of that Climate, and haue obtained of the inhabitants thereof, a certaine winde for twenty dayes together, or the like fixed period of time, according to the distance of place and strings tied with three knots, so that if one were loosed, they should haue a pleasant gale: if the second, a more vehement blast: if the third, such hideous & raging tempests that the Mariners were not able once to looke out, to stand vpon the hatches, to handle their tackle, or to guide the helme with all their strength; and are somtimes violently carried back to the place from whence they first loosed to sea; and many (more hardy then wise) haue bought their triall full deere, opening those knots, and neglecting admonition giuen to the contrary. *Apuleius* ascribeth to *Pamphile*, a Witch of *Thessalia*, little lesse then diuine power to effect strange wonders in heauen, in earth, in hell; to darken the starres, stay the course of riuers, dissolue mountains, and raise vp spirits, this opinion went for currant and vncontrouled. And without all question the Diuell [x] can do this and much more, when God letteth him loose. For he is stiled, *The Prince of the world, Ioh.* 12. 31. *A strong man armed, Luke* 11. 21, *Principality, a ruler of darknesse, spirituall wickednesse in high places, Ephes.* 6. 12.

[x] *De potestate Dæmonum Aquinas in Summa parte* 1. *quest* 110. *Binfeldius in titulum codicis de maleficis & mathematicis. Zanchius de operibus creationis, part.* 1. *lib.* 4. *cap.* 10. 11. 12. *Danæus in Isagoge, parte* 2. *de Angelis bonis & malis.*

Thus he dismaied the heart of *Saul* (when he had

broken the Commandement of God) with dreadfull feare, and enraged his minde with bloudy fury, 1.*Sam*.16 14. Entred into *Iudas*, prouoked him to betray his maister, dispaire and hang himselfe, *Math*. 27. 3. filled the heart of *Ananias* and *Saphira* with dissimulation, *Act*. 5. 3. possessed the bodies of many really, as is manifest in the History of the Gospell. Our Sauiour Christ assureth vs, that a daughter of *Abraham* was bound for 18 yeares by Sathan, with such a spirit of infirmitie, as bowed together, shee could in no wise lift vp her selfe, *Luk*. 13. 11. 16. He spake out of the *Pythonesse*, *Acts* 16. 17. brought downe fire from heauen, and consumed *Iobs* sheepe 7000. and his seruants, raised a storme, strooke the house wherein his sonnes and daughters feasted with their elder brother, smote the foure corners of it, with the ruine whereof they all were destroyed, and perished: and ouerspread the body of that holy Saint their father with botches [y] and biles from the sole of his foot to the crowne of his head. [z] And hee

[y] Vlcus pessimū extensiue quia per totum corpus diffusum, & intensiue, quia in eo omnis morbi & doloris comprehensio vide Mercerum in cap. 2. Iobi.

[z] Regula Theologorum Quæcunque possunt Dæmones possunt etiam magi & malefici eius opera, hinc & illi tempestates excitant Virgilius Ecloga 4ª.

Carmina vel cœlo possunt deducere Lunam:
Carminibus Circe socios mutauit Vlyssis,
Frigidus in pratis cantando rumpitur Anguis, &c.

Et de se Iactans Medea apud Ouidium lib. 7. Metamorphoseōn.

Cum volui ripis ipsis mirantibus; amnes
In fontes rediere suos, concussaque sisto,
Stantia concutio cantu freta, nubila pello,
Nubilaque iudico.

Apud Virgilium Dido Annam sororem alloquitur.

—Mihi Massilæ gentis monstrata sacerdos,
Hæc se carminibus promittit soluere mentes
Sistere aquam fluvijs, & flumina vertere retro.

Et Brachmanius Nonnus Dionysiacon, lib. 36.

ἀἐρινοθὲς καὶ λαγόντες ἐφαρμάξαντο Σελήνην, ἀσταθέες φαέθοντες ἀνεστήσαντο πορείην &c.

De Marco heretico & mago stupenda referunt Ireneus contra hereses. lib. cap. 9. & Epiphanius 3. tom. lib. 1.

will

wil haue his seruants Wisards & Witches, coadiutors with him, and maketh them fit instruments to the performance of all wicked exploits, and this is when God pleaseth (of which I shall haue occasion to speake more afterward) to giue leaue, for his wil is the first supreme and principal cause of all things: and nothing can be done visibly in this Common-wealth here below of the creatures, but is decreed and determined so to be first in the high Court of Heauen, according to his vnsearchable wisedome and iustice, disposing punishments and rewards as seemeth good vnto himselfe. So *Pharaohs* [a] Magitians could turne water into bloud, their roddes into serpents, produce frogges, &c. But when it came to the base vermine, to make lice, they were pusled, and acknowledged their imbecillity, confessing, *Digitus Dei est*, [b] Gods finger is here, *Exod.* 18. 19. For if they could effect and bring to passe all mischieuous designements without his sufferance, it would inferre a weakenesse, and conclude a defect of [c] power in him, as not sufficient to oppose their strength, supplant their force, and auoid their stratagems. And we must not imagine that the practitioners of these damnable Arts of which sexe soeuer, be they men or women, do performe those mischiefes which they effect, by their owne skill, or such meanes as they vse, of which sort bee the bones of dead mens skuls, Toades, Characters, Images, &c. But thorough the cooperation of the Diuell, who is by nature subtile, by long experience instructed, swift to produce

[a] *Iannes, Iambres, 2. Timot. 3*

[b] *Vide Nicolaum Lyranum in & additionem Burgensis, & replicam correctorÿ contra Burgensem.*

[c] *Diabolus Deo perpetuo aduersatur voluntate & actu non semper effectu: id est, Intentio semper est mala, etsi non semper ex animi sui sententia malum perficere possit Deo illud vertente in bonum. Aug. de Ciuit. Dei, lib. cap. 35 & de trinitate lib. 3. cap. 8.*

produceth strange works,& to humane vnderstanding admirable. Yet [d] he will haue those his vassals perswaded of some great benefit bestowed vpon them, whereby they are inabled to helpe and hurt, whom, how, and when they list; and all to indeere them,& by making them partakers in his villany, being strongly bound in his seruice, & stedfastly continued in the same, might more grieuously offend God, and bring iust condemnation vpon themselues. And for the greater, and more forceable inticing allurement hereunto, hee promiseth to giue and doe many things for their sakes, and reueale to them hidden secrets, and future euents, such [e] as he himselfe purposeth to doe, or knoweth by naturall signes shall come to passe. So then to conclude, in [f] euery Magicall action, there must be a concurrence of these three. First, the permitting will of God. Secondly, the suggestion of the Diuell, and his power cooperating. Thirdly, the desire and consent of the Sorcerer; and if [g] any of these be wanting, no trick of witchcraft can be performed. For if God did not suffer it, neither the Diuell, nor the Witch could preuaile to do any thing, no not so much as to hurt one [h] bristle of a Swine. And if the Diuell had not seduced the minde of the wicked woman, no such matter would haue beene attempted. And againe, if hee had not the Witch to bee his instrument, the Diuell were debarred of his purpose.

And as these euill spirits are in themselues different in power, vnderstanding, and subtiltie: so

can

d *Iaquerius in flagello hereticorum fascinariorum, cap. 15.*

e *Augustinus de diuinatione Dæmonum.*

f *Binfeldius de confessionibus maleficorum vnde magorum operationes vim suam habent plenissimam. Aquinas Summa contra gentes, lib. 3. cap. 105. & eius in eum locum commentator Franciscus de Siluestris.*

h *Tritemius in libro responsionum ad quæstiones Maximiliani Imperatoris quæstione.*

Cyrillus Catechismo 4. ad illuminatos, Arbitrium incitare potest Diabolus cogere omnino preter voluntatem non potest.

i *Tertul. de fuga in Persecutione.*

can their seruants do more or lesse through their meanes.

I conclude with that memorable speech of a most noble and learned man,[i] The Diuell is the Author and principall of all that euill which the Witch or Wisard committeth, not thereby to make them more powerfull, but to deceiue them by credulity and ouer-light beliefe, and to get himselfe a companion of his impiety, cruelty, and hatred, which he beareth both to God and man; and also of eternall damnation: for indeed it is his worke, which the foolish and doating wisards coniecture is brought to passe by the words and inchantments which they vtter: and is very busie thus to colour his proceedings, which neuer come abroad in their owne likenesse, because he enuieth the blessed estate of man, and his eternall saluation purchased by the perfect obedience of Christ the Redeemer, and hateth that Image of God which hee beholdeth in him; much like the Panther,[k] who when hee cannot get hold of the man himselfe, is so inflamed with rage, that he teareth his picture in peeces violently which is cast vpon the ground to hinder his pursuit of the hunter who hath carried away his whelpes. And [l] so as *Lactantius* speaketh, these vncleane spirits cast from heauen, wander vp and downe the earth, compasse land and sea, seeking to bring men to destruction as a con fort of their owne desperate and irrecouerable estate.

[i] *Iulius Scaliger de subtilitate, ad Cardanum, exercitatione* 349. *an venefici credulitas vim addat malefico.*

[k] *Basilius Homilia* 21. *in diuersos Scripturæ locos sermone habito in non procul a fine.*

[l] *Lib.* 2. *qui est de origine erroris cap.* 15.

The fourth Propoſition.

HAuing ſhewed before, that the practiſe of Witches receiueth the being and perfection from that [m] agreement which is made betweene them and the Diuell, it now followeth neceſſarily, that we do enquire whether it bee poſſible that there may be any ſuch agreement and league betweene them. The cauſe of doubt ariſeth from the diuerſity or diſparity of their natures, the one being a corporall ſubſtance, the other ſpirituall, vpon which ground ſome [n] haue ſuppoſed that no ſuch contract can paſſe: But we are to hold the contrary affirmatiue, both *de eſſe*, and *de poſſe*, that that there may be, and is, notwithſtanding this difference of eſſence, a mutuall contract of the one with the other: for we read of ſundry leagues between God & his people, and ſome with great ſolemnitie of ceremonies vſed in the ſame, a [o] *Geneſis* 15.9.17. and *Deut*. 5. 2. and in many other like places, yet is hee a ſimple eſſence, [p] free from all diuiſion, multiplication, compoſition, accidents, incorporeall, ſpirituall, and inuiſible. But in Angelicall creatures, though there be no Phyſicall compoſition of matter and forme, or a ſoule and a body; yet is there a metaphyſicall, being ſubſtances conſiſting of an act and poſſibility, ſubiect and accidents. And further, betweene a ſpirit and a man, there is communication of the vnder-

[m] *Nauarrus in Manuali confeſſarior. cap.* 11 *in primum decalogi praeceptum.*

[n] *Ioh. Wierus, totum hoc fictitium putat & foedus imaginarium, & impoſſibile putat, idque paſſim in ſuis libris praecipuè autem de Lamijs, cap.* 7.8. & 23. & *de preſtigijs Daemonũ, lib.*6. *c.* 27, &c. *Hunc refutant eruditè. Binfelde confeſſionibus maleficorum, & Thomas Eraſtus de Lamijs.*

[o] *De his ceremonijs ſimilia, Ier. cap.* 34. 18. & *multa Cyrillus contra Iulianum & Procopius Gazaeus in hunc locum & Auguſtinus.*

[p] *Palanus Syntagmatis Theologiae, l.*2. *cap.* 8.

vnderstanding and will, the faculties and actions whereof must concurre in euery couenant, which is n~thing else but the consent of two or more persons about the thing.

And when the Diuell durst in expresse tearmes tender a contract to our blessed Sauiour, tempting him in the wildernesse, shewing him the kingdomes of the world, and the glory thereof, offered them with this condition, *All these will I giue thee, if thou wilt fall downe and worship me*, *Mat*.4. 9. How much more then will hee aduenture vpon man, weake, wicked, and easie to be seduced? And who [q] can doubt but that these bee the solemne and formall words of a bargaine, *Do vt des, do vt facias*, I giue this for to haue that giuen, I bestow this, to haue such, or such a thing done for me.

Now this couenant is of two sorts, secret or manifest; secret, when one indeuoureth or intendeth to do any thing by such meanes, which neither in nature, nor by institution haue power to produce the purposed effects, or be conioyned as necessary with other, which can bring the same to passe. Expresse, wherein consent is giuen either by writing, and words, or making such signes, whereby they renounce God, and deuote themselues slaues and vassals vnto the Diuell, hee promising, that vpon such condition they shall doe wonders, know future euents, helpe and hurt at their pleasure, and others like vnto these.

An example whereof wee may obserue in [r] *Siluester* the second, one of the holy Fathers of

[q] *Brissonius de formulis, lib.6. Solemnia pactorum sine obligatione verba sunt: spondes? spondeo. promittis? promitto dabis? dabo vt facias, faciam. Iustinianus in institutionibus, lib.3. titulo 16.*

[r] *Hic Monachus Floriacensis cænobij diabolo suadente, & enormiter instigante si eius obsequijs & arti magicæ obligauit in tantum quod Diabolo fecit Homagium cum pacto vt ei omnia ad nutum succederent, &c Holcot. in cap. 17. lib. sapientiæ lectione 190. Platina in illius vita. Vide & Balerum de Romanorum pontificum actis in lib.5. in Syluestro secundo, & Robertum Barnes. de vitis pontificum Romanorum.*

Rome, who did homage to the Diuell his Lord, and made fidelity to liue at his will and appoyntment, vpon condition to obtaine what he desired, by which meanes he got first the Bishopricke of *Rhemes*, after of *Rauenna*, and at the last the Papacie of *Rome*. Which Sea, though it will yeeld good plenty of such like presidents, and we may finde them in authenticall records of Histories, yet I content my selfe with this one.

[f] The formall tearmes of this couenant, as they bee set downe by some, are most dreadfull: and the seuerall poynts these.

[f] *Godelmannus de magia tacita & illicita, lib.1. cap.2. n°. 8. 9. 10 &c.*

To renounce God his Creator, and that promise made in Baptisme.

To deny Iesus Christ, and refuse the benefites of his obedience, yea to blaspheme his glorious and holy name.

To worship the Deuill, & repose all confidence and trust in him.

To execute his commaundements.

To vse things created of God for no end, but to the hurt and destruction of others.

And lastly, to giue himselfe soule and body to that deceitfull and infernall spirit, who on the other part appeareth to them in the shape of a man (which is most common) or some other creature, conferreth familiarly, and bindeth himselfe by many promises, that at all times called for, he will presently come, giue counsell, further their desires, answer any demaund, deliuer from prison, and out of all dangers, bestow riches, wealth, pleasure, and what not? and all without any labour and paines-taking, in a word to become seruiceable to their will, & accomplish all their requests. And this is that which the Prophet *Esay* speaketh, *chap.* 28. 15. to make a couenant with death, and an agreement with hell. The consent of the ancient Fathers, if there were any doubt, might be added to the further clearing of this conclusion. For [t] *Cyprian* directly affirmeth, that all those who vse magicall Arts, make a couenant with the Diuell, yea he himselfe, while he practized the same (before his calling to the light and true knowledge of God) was bound vnto him by an especiall [u] writing, whereunto some subscribe with their owne bloud, which was a vse among diuers nations, and a most sure bond of constant friendship, and [x] inuiolable consociation. But herein these seduced wretches are deceiued: for these promises which he makes, are treacherous, and the obseruances whereunto he enioyneth and perswadeth them, as powerfull in producing such or such effects, meere deceipts, and haue no qualitie in them to that purpose, but respecteth his owne ends, which are one of these foure.

First, to the mouing of them to the breaking of Gods law.

Secondly, to adore him with diuine worship and sacred rites.

Thirdly, to weaken their hope and faith in God.

Fourthly, to couer his owne fraud and treachery, that it may not be perceiued.

And when they finde this Impostor failing in the performance of his vowed promises, then he

[t] *Siue illius sit, siue alterius iste liber. De duplici Martyrio. Aquinas 2[a]. 2a. quest. 96. Iob. Gerson in Trilogio astrologiæ Theologisatæ propositione 21. & de erroribus circa artem magicam, Dicto 2.*

[u] *Camerarius meditationum historiarum, lib. 1. cap. 6. Bodinus exempla ponit Demonomanias. lib. 2. c. 4. Binfeldius de confessionibus maleficorum.*

[x] *Simile de Catilina refert Salustius. cum ad ius iurandum populares sceleris sui adigeret, humani corporis sanguinem vino permixtum in pateris circumtulisse, inde cum post execrationē omnes degustauissent, sicut in solemnibus sacris fieri consueuit aperuisse consiliū suum, atque eo dictitant fecisse, quo inter se magis fidi forent.*

wanteth not his shifts: as that these defects are not to be imputed to him, or the weakenesse of the Art, but their owne negligence or ignorance, who haue not exactly obserued such directions, and in that manner they were deliuered: or mistooke his meaning, which is commonly deliuered in [y] ambiguous tearmes, such as will admit a double construction: and herein appeareth the lamentable and woefull blindnesse of man, who is contented to swallow vp, and excuse many of his lies by one truth fore-told, which hath casually come to passe, whereas in other matters they make light account of, yea cõtemne infinit truths, if they shall finde by long search and diligent inquiry, but one falshood. Wherefore it behoooueth vs to be carefull Centinels ouer our selues, for that our grand [z] aduersary, proud, enuious, and not standing in the truth, reposeth all his possibility of victory in lies, and out of this poysoned sinke, deuiseth all kinde of deceits, that so hee might depriue man of that happy and blessed estate which he lost by pride, and draw him into the society of his owne damnation: therefore it is a needfull caueat giuen by one of the ancient Fathers: Our enemy is old against whom wee

[y] As that to Pope *Siluester* the second, his demand; who asked how long he should liue and enioy the *Popedome*? answered, vntil hee should say masse in *Ierusalem*; and not long after, celebrating the same in a *Chappell* of the Church dedicated to the holy Crosse in *Rome*, called *Ierusalem*, knew how he was ouer-reached, for there hee dyed. And an other paralell to this, may be that of a certaine Bishop, much addicted to these vanities, hauing many enemies, and fearing them, asked the Diuell whether he should fly or not: who answered, *Non, sta secure, venient inimici tui suauiter, & subdentur tibi.* But being surprized, and taken by his aduersaries, and his castle set on fire, expostulating with him, that hee had deceiued him in his distresse, returned answere, that he said true, if his speech had been rightly vnderstood: for he aduised, *Non sta secure* [id est *fugias*] *venient inimici tui suauiter, & subdent vr*, [id est *ignem tibi*]. Such were the Oracles which he gaue, and whereof all histories do testifie. *Holcot* vpon the booke of Wisedome, and the rest before mentioned with him.

[z] *Leo de collectis Serm.* 40. *& natiuitate Domini, Serm.* 7.

fight,

fight, sixe [a] thousand yeares fully compleat are passed since he began to oppose himselfe against vs; but if wee obserue the commandements of God, and continue stedfast in faith, apprehending Iesus Christ, then shall we be able to withstand all his violent assaults, and ouer-come him because Christ in whom we trust, is inuincible.

[a] *In proemio, lib de exhortatione ad Martyrium. Cyprianus.*

The fifth Proposition.

THE Diuell can assume to himselfe [b] a body, and frame a voyce to speake with, and further instruct and giue satisfaction to those who haue submitted themselues vnto him, and are bound to his seruice. For he lost not by his transgression and fall, his naturall [c] endowments, but they continued in him whole [d] and perfect, as in the good Angels, who abide in that obedience and holinesse wherein they were created, from whence a reason confirmatiue may bee thus framed, Good Angels can take vnto themselues bodies, as *Genes.* 18.2. *Iudg.* 13.3.6. therefore the euill also. Thus the Diuell hath appeared to some in the forme of a [e] Man, cloathed in purple, & wearing a crowne vpon his head: to others in the likenesse of a [f] Childe: sometime he sheweth himselfe in the

[b] *Augustinus in Enchiridio, cap .59. & 60. & Lambertus Daneusin suis Commentarijs: ad eundem.*

[c] *Binfeldius de confessionibus maleficorum. Aquinas, Summa part.1.quæst. 51. art.3. & 4*

[d] *In Dęmonibus* ἀγγελικὰς δωρεὰς οὐ μήποτε ἠλλοιῶσθαι φαμὲν, ἀλλὰ εἰσὶ ὁλοκληρεῖς καὶ παμφανεῖς, *Dionisius Areopagita, de diuinis nominibus cap.4. & si vacat licebit consulere in eundem Pachemeræ Paraphrasin & maximi scholia. Isidorus Hispalensis de summo bono. lib.1. cap.12.*

[e] *Sulpitius Seuerus in vita beati Martini. Multa exemplę habet Bodinus in prȩfatione ad Dęmonomaniam.*

[f] *Hieronimus in vita Hilarionis.*

forme

forme of foure-footed beastes, foules, creeping things; [g] roaring as a Lyon, skipping like a Goat, barking after the manner of a dogge, and the like. But [h] it is obserued by some, that he cannot take the shape of a Sheepe, or Doue, though of an Angell of light: 2.*Cor*.11.14. And further, [i] most of the learned doe hold, that those bodies wherein they doe appeare, are fashioned of the [k] aire, (though it is not to be denied, but they can enter into other, as the Diuell did into the Serpent, deceiuing *Eue, Gen*.3.1.) which if it continuing pure and in the owne nature [l], hath neither colour nor figure, yet condensed receiueth both, as wee may behold in the clouds, which resemble sometime one, sometime another shape, and so in them is seene the representation of Armies fighting, of beasts and Birds, houses, Cities, and sundry other kinds of apparations.

Histories of all can witnesse of the Diuels appearance in human [m] shape: thus a *Pseudo-Moses*, or *Messias* in *Crete*, perswaded the Iewes that it was he who brought their Fathers the Israelites out of Egypt, and led them through the Red Sea, and would conduct them also out of that land vpon the waters into *Iudea*. But many following his counsell, perished: the rest admonished by that destruction, turned back, accusing their folly; and when they made enquiry for this guide, to haue rewarded him according to his desert, was no where to be found, whereof they conceiued hee was a Diuell in Mans likenesse. And such an one [n] was that merry (but malicious) spirit, who walked

for

[g] *Psellus de dæmonum natura.*
[h] *Binfeldius de confessionibus maleficorum.*
[i] *Petrus Martyr in 28.caput. lib. 1.Samuelis. Aquinas iu Summa parte 1.quest 51. articul. 2. Hyperius locorũ Theolog. lib.*
[k] *Hesiodus* ἔργων καὶ ἡμερῶν *lib.1.Dæmonas ait esse* ἀέρα ἑσσαμένους. *proclus interpretatur quia sunt corpora aërea*
[l] *Iulius Scaliger de subtilitate ad Cardanum exercitatione 359. sectione 13.*
[m] *Socrates Historiæ ecclesiast. lib.7.cap.38. & historia Tripar- lib.12.cap.9.*
[n] *Chronicon Hirsangiense.*

for a long time in Saxony, and was very seruiceable, clothed in country apparrell, with a cappe on his head, delighted to conuerse and talke with the people, to demaund questions, and answer what he was asked, hurting none, except iniured before, and then declared himselfe a right diuell in reuenge.

[o] The late Discoueries and Nauigations made into the west Indies, can furnish vs with abundant testimonies hereof, in which the mindes of the Inhabitants are both terrified & their bodies massacred by his visible sight, and cruell tortures; yet (which is the opinion of many learned) he cannot so perfectly represent the fashion of a mans body, but that there is some sensible deformity, by which hee bewrayeth himselfe; as his [p] feete like those of an Ox, a Horse, or some other beasts, clouen houed, his hands crooked, armed with clawes, or talants like a vulture: or some one misshapen part, wherein (though hee delight in the shape of man, as most fitting for company and conference) is demonstrated, the great and tender loue of God toward vs, who hath so branded this deceiuer, that hee may bee discerned euen of those who are but of meane capacity, and so consequently auoyded. And as in his body assumed, so in his speech there is a defect, for it is weake, small, whispering, imperfect.

And thus it is [q] reported of *Hermolaus Barbarus*, who inquiring of a spirite, the signification and meaning of a difficult [r] word in *Aristotle*, he

[o] *Vide nauigationē Monsieur de Monts, ad nouam Franciam, lib. 2. cap. 5.*

[p] *Binfeldius de confessionibus maleficorum. Alexander ab Alexandro dierum Genialium, lib. 1. cap. 19. Remigius de Demonolatria, lib. 1. cap. 7. & apud Rhodingium antiquarum lectionum lib. 29. cap. 5. est exemplum dignum admiratione.*

[q] *Remigius demonolatrias lib. 1. cap. 8 & simile commemorat de Appione Grammatico Plinius naturalis histor. lib. 30. cap. 2. Nicephorus lib. 5. sub finem.*

[r] ἐντελέχεια.

he hard a low hissing, and murmuring voyce giuing answere.

And this hee doth of set purpose, that so his sophisticall & doubtfull words might be the lesse perceiued.

Neither can this seeme strange to any, that the Diuell should speake, who brought a voyce from Trees to salute [f] *Apollonius*, and inspired that talkatiue Oke in *Dodona*, famous for the Oracles vttered there in Heroicall verse, to the Grecians, and to euery nation in his owne language, Chaldeans, Egyptians, Armenians, and other people who were led by him, and depended vpon his resolution.

[f] *Philostratus de vita Apollonij lib.6.cap.13.*

And thus the [t] Image of *Memnon*, when the Sunne did shine vpon it, and his beames touched the lips thereof, (which was at the arising in the East) speake vnto them who were present.

And considering, as hath beene mentioned before, that there passeth betweene the Witch and her Diuell, a compact, as with a Maister and a Seruant, it must therefore consist vppon prescript tearmes of commaunding, and obeying; and then of necessity is required a conuersing together; and conference whereby the same couenant may be ratified.

[t] *Sophocles in Trachinijs vacat* δρῦν πολυγλωσσον, *quia vt eius Scholiastes interpretatur* ἤτοι πολλὰ μαντευομένης, καὶ διὰ τοῦτο πολλὰ φθεγγομένης, ἢ τῆς διαφόροις διαλέκτοις χρησμῳδούσης καὶ κατὰ τὴν ἑκάστου τῶν μαντευομένων γλῶσσαν. *Et hinc Argo Lycophron in Alexandra sua* λαλήθεσν κισσαν *nominat quæ ex Didonea quercu malum habuisse traditur quæ aliquoties locuta est vt apud Apollonium Argonauticõn quarto ideo &* ἰύλαλον Ἀργω *Orpheus appellat, vide plura apud Strabonem lib. 17. & eius de hoc sono iudicium perpende. Pausanias in descriptione decem regionum veteris Græciæ, libro primo in Atticis. Iuuenalis Satyro 15. Psellus de Dæmonum natura. Tacitus libro secundo Annalium.*

The

The sixt Proposition.

GOd giueth, both the diuell, and his seruants the witches, power sometimes to trouble his owne children; so [u] Christ our blessed Sauiour, was by Sathan carryed from place to place, *Math.* 4.5. *Iob* [x] in strange manner afflicted, and his children slaine, through his power, whom none can conceiue but were Gods seruants, religiously brought vp in his feare: and their father hath an honourable testimonie from the mouth of God himselfe, *Iob* 1.*ver*.8. *Dauid*, a man according to Gods owne heart, *Acts* 13.22. is by Sathan stirred vp to number the people, 1.*Chron*. 21.1. and that in curiosity and the pride of his heart, onelie to know the multitude of his subiects, 2.*Sam*.24.2

Whereas the Law appoynteth another end, *Exod*. 30.12. which hee had [y] now forgotten, the maintenance of the Ministerie and worshippe of God. And a daughter of *Abraham* is bound of the diuell eighteene whole yeeres, had a spirit of Infirmity, was bowed together, and could in no wise lift vp herselfe, *Lu*. 13.11.16. a grieuous calamity in respect of the author, the coutinuance, and the effect. But to handle this poynt a little more distinctly; It shall not be amisse to open first some reasons, why God doth giue this power to the diuel ouer the righteous his children sometimes, as also vpon the wicked and disobedient to his

[u] *Iaquerius in flagello hereticorum fascinariorum, cap.* 19. & 20.

[x] *Binfeldius de confessionibus maleficorum.*

[y] *Iosephus* ἀρχαιολογίας *lib*.7. *sectione siue capite iuxta Græcam editionem* 10.

his will: And in the second place, why Witches haue the like leaue graunted vnto them. Therefore for his children.

The first reason of his permission is his inscrutable [y] wisedome, who out of euill bringeth good; so *Paul* had a minister of Sathan to buffet him, to keepe him in humility, that hee might not waxe proude and high-minded, in regard of those great mysteries which were reuealed when hee was taken into the third heauen, 2.*Corint*.12.4. Thus his tentation was a medicine preseruatiue preuenting the disease of his soule, which otherwise hee might haue falne into, [z] for both himselfe, and the rest of the Apostles, though they were chosen vessells, yet were they also fraile and brittle, wandring yet in the flesh vpon earth, not triumphing securely in heauen.

Second, It is [a] proceeding from his mercy and goodnes, for the trial of faith, obedience and constancy in such as belong to God: whereof there is an excellent patterne, and vnparaleld in *Iob* 1. 13.14.*&c.* for by this triall is made a proofe to examine whether wee doe continue firme vpon our square, and vnshaken, or no; and be not remoued, eyther by the [b] seeming wonders of the diuell, or of his seruants and associats. And therefore the Apostle pronounceth him blessed, who endureth temptation, for when hee is tryed hee shall receiue the crowne of life, which the Lord hath promised to them that loue him, *Iames* 1.12. for he is faithfull, and wil not suffer vs to be tempted aboue that we are able, but with the temptati-

[y] *Zanchius de operibus creationis.part.1.lib.4.cap.13.apud quem etiam plura inuenies.Tertul.de fuga in persecutione has causas ponit permissionis diuinæ, aut ex causa probationis conceditur diabolo vis tentationis prouocato, vel prouocanti, aut ex causa reprobationis traditur ei peccator aut ex causa cohibitionis, vt Apostolus refert sibi datum angelum Satanæ.*

[z] *Beda in collectaneis ex Augustino ad Epistolas Pauli.*

[a] *Iaquerius in flagello hereticorum fascinariorum, cap.*20.

[b] *Ceolcenus* δοκιμάζεται ἡ ἡμετέρα ὀρθόδοξος πίστις εἰ ἑδραία ἐστὶ καὶ πάγια προσμένουσα τῷ κυρίῳ, καὶ μὴ ὑποσυρομένη ὑπὸ τοῦ ἐχθροῦ, διὰ τῶν φαντασιωδῶν τεράτων καὶ σατανικῶν ἔργων, τῶν πραττομένων ὑπὸ τῶν δούλων καὶ ὑπηρετῶν κακίας.

on alſo make away to eſcape, &c. 1.*Cor.* 10.13.

Third, Wee are admoniſhed alwayes to ſtand in a readines, and be armed for to fight, prepared to withſtand the diuell, knowing that God doth oftentimes giue him leaue to aſſault vs. Therefore we haue need to be furniſhed in all points, for we wraſtle not againſt fleſh and blood, but againſt principalities, againſt powers, againſt the rulers of the darkeneſſe of this world, againſt ſpirituall wickedneſſes in high places, *Epheſ.*6.11.12. And 1.*Pet.* 5.8. 9. be ſober and vigilant, becauſe your aduerſary the diuell as a roaring Lyon walketh about, ſeeking whom he may deuoure. He [d] is no weake aſſaylant, and therefore heere by the Apoſtle are noted in him foure things: Firſt, his power (a Lyon): Second, his hatred, and wrath in the word (roaring): Third, his ſubtilty (walking about) obſeruing euery oportunity and occaſion to hurt vs: Fourth, his cruelty (deuoure) no contentment but in our ruine and vtter deſtruction.

[d] *Strigelius in explicatione locorum Theologicorum Melanthonis parte* 3. *titulo de cruce & calamitatibus.*

Fourth, God would haue vs get the victorie againſt Sathan, and take knowledge, that Chriſt on our ſide fighteth for vs, through whom we triumph, and ſo are made more vndoubtedly aſſured of our ſaluation; and this is that which hee promiſed, *The* [e] *Seed of the woman ſhall bruiſe the head of the Serpent, Gen.* 3.15. And the Apoſtle confirmeth, God ſhall tread downe Sathan vnder your feete, *Rom.* 16.20.

[e] *Auguſtinus de Geneſi ad literam, l.*11. *c.* 22.

God ſuffereth the diuell to preuaile againſt the wicked, yet in the moſt Holy there is no iniuſtice 2.*Chron.*19.7. But

[f] *Hyperius in locis Theolog. lib.2*

[g] *Augustinus in locum consula.tur.*

[h] *Vide Iaquerium in flagello hereticorum fascinariorum, cap. 23.*

[i] *Idem cap.21.*

First, [f] Herein is the declaration of his iustice, whereby hee punisheth obstinate sinners, & those who prouoke him to wrath, and will not repent: And thus it is sayd of the *Aegiptians*, whom no plagues could soften, that hee cast vpon them the fiercenes of his anger, and indignation, and trouble, by sending euill Angels among them, [g] *Psalm* 78.49. And when *Saul* had neglected the commandement of God, an euill spirit from the Lord troubled him, 1.*Sam.* 16.14. Thus *Ahab* seduced by his false prophets descendeth into the battaile, and is slaine (contemning the words of *Michaiah*) in [h] whose mouthes the diuell was a lying spirit, who sent of the Lord, perswaded him and preuailed, 1.*Kin.*22.22.23.24.

Second, By affliction in the body or goodes, God [i] would quicken them vp to seeke the saluation of their soules. And so *Paul* gaue ouer a scandalous and incestuous person vnto the diuell, that he might be induced to forsake his sin, liue chastely heereafter, and be an edifying example to those whom he had offended: and this kinde of discipline was more soueraigne, then any other could haue beene, because mans nature abhorreth Sathan, and trembleth with feare once to conceiue that he should fall into his power and hands, and this is that which he writeth, aduising the Corinthians to deliuer him vnto Sathan, for the destruction of the flesh, that the spirit may be saued in the day of the Lord Iesus, 1.*Cor.*5.5. And in this sort he speaketh of two other deceiuers and blasphemers, *Hymenaus* and *Alexander*, I haue deliuered

red

red them vnto Sathan, that they may learne not to blaspheme, 1.*Timothie* 1.20. therfore this giuing ouer, was not to destruction, but for correction.

The last poynt propounded, was, That witches haue power granted to vex Gods owne children aswell as others, and preuaile ouer them; and that we doe enquire (so farre as we may, and is iustifiable) of the causes thereof, which may be these.

First, [i] This is permitted vnto them for the experience of their faith and integrity, so that by this meanes their loue towards God which lay hidden in the heart, is now made manifest. To be quiet and patient in prosperity, when we may enioy benefites at our owne pleasure, is a matter easily to be performed: But to endure the fire of Tribulation, that is the proofe of a stedfast Christian, and in losses and sickenesse procured by such to bee silent, and submit our selues, this is the note of a faithfull man, & to choose rather obeying the law of God, to beare the infirmity of the body, then to ouer-flow in riches, and enioying health and strength offend the Lord.

[k] *Trithemius in libel.8.quæstionum quas illi dissoluendas proposuit Maximilianus Imperator, quæst 7.*

Second, this maketh a difference betweene the wicked and the godly: for thus the holy Apostle speaketh of the righteous, that by many afflictions they must enter into the kingdome of heauen, *Act.* 14.22. And all that will liue godly in Christ Iesus suffer tribulations, 2. *Timoth.* 3.12. for whom the Lord loueth, he doth chasten, *Prouer.* 3.12. It is a Christians glory to vndergoe for Gods cause, any vexation whatsoeuer, whether wrought by the

diuell,

[k] *Potestatis diabolo concesse has causas ponit Iohannes Gerson de erroribus circa artem magicam, in dicto secundo.*
1°. *Obstinatorum damnationem.*
2°. *Peccatorum purgationem, & punitionem.*
3°. *Ad fidelium probationem, & exercitationem.*
4° *Ad gloriæ dei manifestationem*

diuell, or brought to passe by wicked men his [k] instruments; for when he is tryed, hee shall receiue the crowne of life, which God hath promised to those who loue him, *Iames* 1.12. But wee reade contrary of the wicked, they become olde, yea, are mighty in power, their seede is established in their sight with them, and their of-spring before their eyes, their houses are safe from feare, neyther is the rod of God vpon them, &c. they spend their dayes in wealth, and in a moment go downe into the graue, *Iob* 21.7.8.9. &c. Yet surely they are set in slippery places, sodainely destroyed and perished, & horribly consumed as a dreame when one awaketh: O Lord, thou shalt make their Image despised, &c. *Psal.* 73.18.19.20.

The seuenth Proposition.

[l] *In Perkei abbboth. Bodinus in confutatione opinionis Wieri. Plinius in hist. natural. Quintilianus Institutionum oratoriarium lib.5.cap. 10.*

MOre women in a farre different proportion prooue Witches then men, by a hundred to one; therefore the Lawe of God noteth that Sex, as more subiect to that sinne, *Exodus* 22.18. It is a common speach amongst the Iewish Rabbins, [l] many women, many Witches: And it should seeme that this was a generally receiued opinion, for so it is noted by *Pliny*, *Quintilian*, and others, neyther doth this proceede (as some haue thought) from their frailtie and imbecillity, for in many of them there is stronger resolution, to vndergoe any torment then can bee found in man,

man, as was made apparant in that conspiracy of *Piso* against *Nero*, [m] who commannded that *Epicharis*, knowne to bee of the same faction, should first presently be set vpon the racke, imagining that being a woman, she would neuer bee able to ouercome the paine: But all the tortures that he or his could deuise, were not able to draw from her the least confession of any thing that was then obiected against her. The first dayes question shee so vtterly contemned, that the very Chaire in which they conueied her from the place, did seeme as a Chariot wherein shee rid, triumphing ouer the barbarous vsage of their inhumane cruelty. The morrow following brought thither againe, after many rough incounters, remained so vnshaken, that wrath it selfe grew madde, to see the strokes of an obstinate and relenting fury fall so in vaine vpon the softer temper of a Woman: and at the last tooke a scarfe from about her necke, and by it knits vp within her bosome the knowledge shee had of that fact, together with that little remainder of spirit, whereof by force and violence they laboured to depriue her.

[m] *Tacit. Annal. lib.15.*

Muliebre corpus impar dolori.

[n] Former ages haue likewise produced *Leena* an exemplary president of this sort, to all posterity, who when *Armodius* and *Aristogiton* hauing failed of the execution of their enterprise against *Hipparchus* a tyrant, had beene put to death, she was brought to the torture to be enforced to declare what other complices there were of the conspiracie. But rather then shee

[n] *Tertul. in Apologet. Crinitus de doctrina Christiana lib.9. cap.8.*

should bee compelled thereunto, bit her tongue asunder, and spit it in the face of the tyrant, that though she would, yet could not now disclose them. In remembrance whereof the Athenians caused a Lyon of Brasse to bee erected, shewing her inuincible courage by the generosity of that beast, and her perseuerance in secrecie, in that they made it without a tongue. Therefore the learned haue searched out other causes thereof, and among the rest, obserued these as the most probable.

First, they are by nature credulous, wanting experience, and therfore more easily deceiued.

Secondly, ° they harbour in their breast a curious and inquisitiue desire to know such things as be not fitting and couenient, and so are oftentimes intangled with the bare shew and visard of goodnesse. As the Lady of Rome, who was importune, and vehemently instant vpon her husband, to know what was debated of that day at the Councell Table. And when he could not be at rest, answered, The Priests had seene a Larke flying in the aire with a golden Helmet on his head, and holding a speare in his foot. Scarce she had this, but presently she told it to one of her maids: she to another of her fellowes, so that report was spread through the whole Citie, and went for currant vntill it receiued a checke: But all are not of this mould.

° Binfeldius de confessionibus maleficorum. Peucerus de precipuis diuinationum generibus in titulo de θεομαντεία. Martinus de Arles.

Thirdly, their complection is softer, and from hence more easily receiue the impressions offered by the Diuell; as when they be instructed and gouerned

uerned by good Angels, they proue exceeding religious, and extraordinarily deuout: so consenting to the suggestions of euill spirits, become notoriously wicked, so that there is no mischiefe aboue that of a woman, *Eccles.* 25.13.&c.

Fourthly, in them is a greater facility to fall, and therefore the Diuell at the first tooke that aduantage, and set vpon *Eue* in *Adams* absence, *Genes.* 3.3.

Fifthly, this sex, when it conceiueth wrath or hatred against any, is vnplacable, possessed with vnsatiable desire of reuenge, and transported with appetite to right (as they thinke) the wrongs offered vnto them: and when their power herein answereth not their will, and are meditating with themselues how to effect their mischieuous proiects and designes, the Diuell [p] taketh the occasion, who knoweth in what manner to content exulcerated mindes, windeth himselfe into their hearts, offereth to teach them the meanes by which they may bring to passe that rancor which was nourished in their breasts, and offereth his helpe and furtherance herein.

[p] *Exemplum apud Binfeldium reperies de confessionibus maleficorum, pag.* 32.

Sixthly, they are of a slippery tongue, and full of words: and therefore if they know any such wicked practises, are not able to hold them, but communnicate the same with their husbands, children, consorts, and inward acquaintance; who not considerately weighing what the issue and end thereof may be, entertaine the same, and so the poyson is dispersed. Thus *Dalilah* discouered her husbands strength where it lay, vnto the Philiſtines; and procured his infamous and diſaſtrous ouer-throw. *Iudg.* 16.18.

Hitherto in ſome Popoſitions I haue ſet downe the originall of witch-craft, and other ſuch curious and vnlawfull Arts, the quality of the perſons agents in the ſame, the power of the Diuell, and his confederates, the league of aſſociation which enterchangeably paſſeth betweene them, his aſſuming a body, and framing a voice for the performance of that buſineſſe; that women, and why, are moſt ſubiect to this helliſh practiſe. Now the truth of all theſe ſhall appeare by exemplary proofes in the Narration following.

A true Narration of ſome of thoſe *Witch-crafts which* Marie *wife of* Henry Smith Glouer did practiſe, and of the *hurts ſhe hath done vnto ſundry perſons by the ſame:* confirmed by her owne Confeſſion, and from the pub-*like Records of the examination of diuers vpon their oaths:* of her death, and execution for the ſame, which *was on the twelfth day of Ianuarie laſt paſt.*

M*Arie* wife of *Henrie Smith*, Glouer, poſſeſſed with a wrathfull indignation againſt ſome of her neighbours, in regard that they made gaine of their buying and ſelling Cheeſe, which ſhee (vſing the ſame trade) could not doe, or they better (at the leaſt in her opinion) then ſhe did, often times curſed them, and became incenſed with vnruly paſſions, armed with a ſetled reſolution, to effect ſome miſchie-

uous

uous proiects and designes against them. The diuell who is skilfull, and reioyceth of such an occasion offered, and knoweth how to stirre vp the euill affected humours of corrupt mindes (she becomming now a fitte subiect, through this her distemper, to worke vpon, hauing the vnderstanding darkened with a cloude of passionate, and reuengefull affections) appeared vnto her amiddes

Proposition 4. these discontentments, in the shape of a blacke man, and willed that she should continue in her malice, enuy, hatred, banning and cursing; and then he would be reuenged for her vpon all those

Proposition 5. to whom she wished euill: and this promise was vttered in a lowe murmuring and hissing voyce: and at that present they entred tearmes of a compact, he requiring that she should forsake God, and depend vpon him: to which she condescended in expresse tearmes, renouncing God, and betaking herselfe vnto him. I am sparing by anie amplification to enlarge this, but doe barely and nakedly rehearse the trueth, and number of her owne words vnto mee. After this hee presented himselfe againe at sundry times, and that to this purpose (as may probably bee coniectured) to hold her still in his possession, who was not able, eyther to looke further into these subtilties, then the superficiall barke thereof, or not discouer the depth of his designements, and in other formes, as of a mist, and of a ball of fire, with some dispersed spangles of blacke; and at the last in prison (after the doome of iudgement, and sentence of condemnation was passed against her) two seuerall

times,

times, in that figure as at the first: only at the last he seemed to haue a paire of horns vpon his head, and these as shee came downe from her chamber, being sent for to conferre with some learned and reuerend Diuiues, by whose prayers and instructions she might be brought to the sight and confession of her grieuous offences, be regained and rescued out of his hands, brought to repentance, and the fauour of God, assured hope of mercie, and eternall life, and at these times he wished her to confesse nothing to any of them, but continue constant in her made promise, rely vpon him, and hee would saue her. This was too high a straine aboue his reach to haue made it good, and a note of his false descant, who hauing compassed this wretched woman, brought her to a shamefull and vntimely end; yet doing nothing herein contrary to his malicious purposes, for hee was a murtherer from the beginning, *Iohn* 8.44. Now then, to descend to particulars, and the effects of this hellish association made!. Being thus ioyned and linked together in a reciprocall league, he beginneth to worke for her, in procuring the mischiefe of those whom she maligned, whereof these few acknowledged by her selfe, may yeeld some taste of more, though concealed.

Her

¶ *Her wicked practise against Iohn Orkton.*

THe first who tasted of the gall of her bitternes was *Iohn Orkton* a Sailer, and a man of strong constitution of body, who about some fiue yeares sithence, returning out of Holland in the Netherland, or low Countries beyond the Seas, happened, for some misdemeanors committed by him to strike the sonne of this *Mary Smith* (but in such sort as could not in reason bee offensiuely taken) who hearing his complaint, came foorth into the streete, cursing and banning him therefore, as oftentimes shee did, dwelling in the next adioyning house, and wished in a most earnest and bitter manner, that his fingers might rotte off; wherevpon presently hee grew weake, distempered in stomacke, and could digest no meate, nor other nourishment receiued, and this discrasie or feeblenesse continued for the space of three quarters of a yeare; which time expired, the fore-mentioned griefe fel downe from the stomacke into his hands and feete, so that his fingers did corrupt, and were cut off; as also his toes putrified & consumed in a very strange and admirable manner. Neuerthelesse, notwithstanding these calamities, so long as hee was able, went still to Sea, in the goods and shippes of sundry Merchants (for it

was

was his onely meanes of liuing) but neuer could make any prosperous voyage (as then other men did) eyther beneficiall to the Owners, or profitable to him selfe. Whereupon, not willing to bee hindrance to others, and procure no good for his owne maintenance by his labours, left that trade of life, and kept home, where his former griefe encreasing, sought to obtaine help and remedie by Chirurgery , and for this end went to Yarmouth, hoping to be cured by one there, who was accompted very skilfull: but no medicines applyed by the Rules of Arte and Experience, wrought any expected or hoped for effect: for both his hands and feete, which seemed in some measure euery euening to be healing, in the morning were found to haue gone backeward, and growne far worse then before: So that the Chirurgian perceiuing his labour to bee wholly frustrate, gaue ouer the cure, and the diseased patient still continueth in a most distressed and miserable estate, vnto the which hee was brought by the hellish practises of this malitious woman, who long before openly in the streetes, (whenas yet the neighbours knew of no such thing) reioycing at the calamity, said, *Orkton* now lyeth a rotting. And no maruell though she could tell that which herselfe had done, and her good maister would not suffer to be concealed, but that the testimony of her owne tongue should remayne as a record towardes her further detection and condemnation, who sought meanes of her voluntary accord to be reconciled with the wofull distressed party, but this was nothing else but to plaister ouer and disguise her former inhumane and barbarous actions, for no reliefe at all followed thereof: for oftentimes, as hath beene prooued, the [a] diuells and witches his instruments doe cause such diseases, which neyther the one, nor the other can remoue againe. And this is not any vaporous imagination, but a most vndoubted trueth. For now this poore man continueth still in a lamentable estate, griefe, and paines encreasing, without hope of helpe, except God in the abundance of his tender mercies vouchsafe to grant comfort and deliuerance.

[a] Propositiõ 3.

¶ *Her wicked practise against Elizabeth Hancocke.*

THe second person distressed, by this witch, was *Elizabeth Hancocke*, then widdow, now wife of *Iames Scot*: the maner, occasion, and proceeding of whose dealing against her was thus. She comming out of the towne from the shoppe of one *Simon Browne* a Silkeman, vnto whom she had carried home some worke, which was by him put out vnto her; *Henry Smith*, as shee passed by his doore, tooke her by the hand, and smilingly said, that his ducke (meaning his wife, this woman of whom we now speake) tolde him that shee had stolne her henne; which wordes shee then passed

ouer,

ouer, as onely ſpoken in merriment, and denying the ſame : in the meane time, as they were interchanging theſe words, ſhee came herſelfe, and directly charged her with the henne, and wiſhed that the bones thereof might ſticke in her throat, when ſhe ſhould eate the ſame : which ſpeech alſo ſhe made no great reckoning of, ſuppoſing them to be but words of courſe, and might bee vttered in jeaſt. Neuertheleſſe, afterward better conſidering of the ſame, conceiued much griefe, to bee counted one of ſo euill quality and diſpoſition, and eſpying that hen for which ſhe was accuſed, to ſit vpon the hatch of her ſhoppe doore, went to her, and mooued with the indignity of that ſlaunder, and vniuſt imputation, told her in ſome paſſion and angry manner, that it was a diſhoneſt part thus to blemiſh the good name of her neighbors with ſo vntrue aſperſions: whereupon, breaking foorth in ſome violence, ſhe wiſhed the pox to light vpon her, and named her prowde *Iinny*, prowde flurts, and ſhaking the hand, bade her go in, for ſhe ſhould repent it; and the ſame night, within three or foure houres after theſe curſes and imprecations vttered, ſhe was taken and pinched at the heart, and felt a ſodaine weakneſſe in all the parts of her body; yet her appetite to meate nothing diminiſhed, and ſo continued for the ſpace of three weekes; in which time, when ſhe was any thing well, would come to the doore, and leane vpon the ſtall, whom this *Marie Smith* ſeeing, did euer banne, adding the former curſe, the poxe light vpon you, can you yet come to the doore?

and at the end of these three weekes, beeing but very weake, came foorth as shee vsed to doe, to take the ayre, this mischieuous woman most bitterly cursed her againe, whereupon she went into the house, fell into such a torturing fit, and nipping at the heart, that she fainted, hardly recouerable for the space of halfe an houre, and so grieuously racked and tormented through all parts of her body, as if the very flesh had beene torne from the bones, by the violent paine whereof she could not refraine, but tore the haire from off her head, and became as one distraught, bereaued of sence, and vnderstanding: And the same night the bed whereon she lay, was so tossed, and lifted vp and downe, both in her owne feeling, and in the sight of others then present beholders of her extreamities, by the space of one houre or more, that she was therewith exceedingly terrified, & did thinke oftentimes in her sleepe, that she did see this *Marie Smith* standing before her. And this fit continued sixteene houres, during which passion *Edward Drake* her father came to the Towne, touched with griefe for this torture of his daughter (as parents hearts are relenting and tender, and naturall compassion is soone stirred vp in them) tooke her vrine, went to one for his aduice (whose fact herein is no way instifiable, and argued but a small measure of religion, and the knowledge of God in him) who first tolde vnto him the cause of his comming, that is, to seeke help for his daughter, and then added, that she was so farre spent, that if hee had stayed but one day longer, the woman

who

who had wrongd her, would haue ſpent her heart, and ſo become vnrecouerable, and thereupon ſhewed him her face in a Glaſſe; and further, opened the beginning cauſe of falling out, which was for a hen, which before this, *Drake* neyther knew nor heard of, and then gaue his counſell for remedy, which was the matter ſought for & deſired, & that was in this order. To make a cake with flower from the Bakers, & to mix the ſame inſtead of other liquor, with her own water, and bake it on the harth, wherof the one halfe was to be applyed and laid to the region of the heart, the other halfe to the back directly oppoſit; & further, gaue a box of ointment like triacle, which muſt be ſpread vpon that cake, and a powder to be caſt vpon the ſame, and certaine words written in a paper, to be layd on likewiſe with the other, adding this caueat, that if his daughter did not amend within ſix houres after the taking of theſe receits, then there was no health or recouery to be looked for: & further, wiſhed ſilence to be kept herein, for the womā who had done this, would know any thing.

And being thus furniſhing with inſtructions, and returning home, as hee alighted from his horſe to enter into that houſe where his daughter lay (being the next vnto *Mary Smiths*) ſhee then ſtood leaning ouer her ſhop window, whom hee knew to be that perſon, which was ſhewed vnto him, and ſhe curſed him paſſing by, and told his daughter that her Father had beene with a Wiſard. And the next day following after they had put in practiſe the directions giuen, ſhe affirmed to diuers of the neighbours, that *Drake* the afflicted womans father, had beene to aske counsell, and made a Witch Cake, but shee would learne how they came to haue that knowledge: yet for the present she found helpe, and was freed from the languishing and other conflicts wherewith she was assaulted by the space of sixe weekes.

After this, being married vnto *Iames Scot*, a great Cat which kept with this Witch (of whose infernall both purposes and practises wee now speake) frequented their house; and vpon doing some scathe, her husband moued therwith, thrust it twice through with his sword: which notwithstanding those wounds receiued, ran away: then he stroke it with all his force vpon the head with a great pike staffe, yet could not kill her; but shee leapt after this vpward almost a yard from the boords of that chamber where she now was, and crept downe: which hee perceiuing, willed his lad (a boy of foureteene yeares) to dragge her to the muck-hill, but was not able; and therefore put her into a sacke, and being in the same, still moued and stirred. Whereupon they put her out againe, and cast her vnder a paire of staires, purposing in the morning, to get more helpe, and carry her away; but then could not be found, though all the doores that night were locked, and neuer heard what afterward became thereof.

Not long after, this Witch came forth with a Birchin broome, and threatned to lay it vpon the head of *Elizabeth Scot*, and defiled her cloathes therewith, as she swept the street before her shop doore

doore, and that in the sight of her husband, who not digesting this indignity offered vnto his wife, threatned that if she had any such fits, as she endured being a Widow before marriage, hee would hang her. At this she clapped her hands, and said hee killed her Cat. And within two or three dayes after this enterchange of words betweene them, his wife was perplexed with the like paine and griefe at her heart, as formerly she had beene; and that for two dayes and a night: wherefore her husband went to this wrathfull and malicious person, assuring that if his wife did not amend, hee would accuse her to the Magistrate, and cause the *rigor of the law to be executed vpon her, which is due to such malefactors. These things were done some three yeares sithence. The party troubled yet liueth, but in no confirmed health, nor perfect soundnesse of body.

** Witches can by no meanes bee so easily brought to recall the mischiefe they haue done, as by threats and stripes. Remigius in Dæmonolatria, lib 3. c. 3.*

Her wicked practises against Cicely Balye.

A Third subiect whereupon this wrathfull womans anger wrought, was *Cicely Balye*, then seruant to *Robert Coulton*, now wife of *William Vaux*, who sweeping the street before her maisters doore vpon a Saturday in the euening, *Mary Smith* began to pick a quarrell about the manner of sweeping, and said vnto her she was a great fat-tail'd sow, but that fatnesse should shortly be pulled

led downe and abated. And the next night being Sunday immediatly following, a Cat came vnto her, sate vpon her breast, with which she was grieuously tormented, and so oppressed, that she could not without great difficulty draw her breath, and at the same instant did perfectly see the said *Mary* in the chamber where she lay, who (as she conceiued) set that Cat vpon her, and immediatly after fell sicke, languished, and grew exceeding leane; and so continued for the space of halfe a yeare together, during the whole continuance in her maisters seruice; vntill departing from him, she dwelt with one Mistres *Garoway*, and then began to bee amended in her health, and recouer of her former pining sicknesse: for this Witch had said, that so long as she dwelt neere her, she should not be well, but grow from euill to worse.

Thus euery light trifle (for what can bee lesse then sweeping of a little dust awry?) can minister matter to set on fire a wrathfull indignation, and inflame it vnto desired reuenge, the Diuell being willing to apprehend and take hold vpon such an occasiō, that so he might do some pleasing office to his bond-slaue, whō she adored in submisse maner, vpon her knees, with strange gestures, vttering many murmuring, broken, and imperfect speeches, as this *Cicely* did both heare and see, there being no other partition between the chamber wherein shee performed these rites, and the house of her maister with whom she then dwelt, but only a thin seeling of boord, through a cranny or rift whereof she looked, listned attentiuely vnto her words, and beheld (diligently her behauiour, and might haue seene and heard much more, but that she was with the present spectacle so affrighted, that shee hastned downe in much feare and distemper.

Her wicked practise against Edmund Newton.

THe fourth endammaged by this Hagge, was one *Edmund Newton* : the discontentment did arise from this ground ; Because hee had bought seuerall bargaines of Holland cheese, and sold them againe, by which she thought her benefit to be somewhat impaired, vsing the like kinde of trading. The manner of her dealing with him was in this sort. At euery seuerall time of buying Cheese he was grieuously afflicted, being thrice, and at the last, either she or a spirit in her likenesse did appeare vnto him, and whisked about his face (as he lay in bed) a wet cloath of very loathsome sauour ; after which hee did see one cloathed in russet with a little bush beard, who told him hee was sent to looke vpon his sore legge, and would heale it ; but rising to shew the same, perceiuing hee had clouen feet, refused that offer, who then (these being no vaine conceits, or phantasies, but well aduised and diligently considered obseruances) suddenly vanished out of sight. After this she sent her Impes, a Toad, and Crabs crawling about the house, which was a shoppe planchered with boords, where his seruants (hee being a Shooemaker) did worke: one of which tooke that toad, put it into the fire, where it made a groaning noyse for one quarter of an houre before it was consumed; during which time *Mary Smith* who sent it, did endure, (as was reported) torturing paines, testifying the felt griefe by her out-cryes then made.

The sicknesse which he first sustained, was in manner of a madnesse or phrensie, yet with some interposed release of extremity: so that for thirteene or foureteene weekes together hee would be of perfect memory, other times distracted and depriued of all sence. Also the ioynts and parts of his body were benummed, besides other pains and greifes from which hee is not yet freed, but continueth in great weakenesse, disabled to performe any labour, whereby hee may get sufficient and competent maintenance. And by the councel of some, sending for this woman by whom hee was wronged, that he might scratch her (for this hath gone as currant, and may plead prescription for warrant a foule sinne among Christians to thinke one Witch-craft can driue out another) his nailes turned like feathers, hauing no strength to lay his hands vpon her.

And it is not improbable but that she had dealt no better with others then these aboue mentioned. For Mr *Thomas Tonges* of London, Fishmonger, reported vnto me, that after the demand of a debt due vnto M[r] *Iohn Mason*, Silkeman of the ſame Citie, whoſe Widow hee married, from *Henry Smith* Glouer her husband, ſome execrations and curſes being wiſhed vnto him, within three or foure dayes (being then gone to Yarmouth in Norfolke vpon neceſſary buſineſſe) there fell ſicke, and was tortured with exceeding and maſſacring griefes, which by no meanes (hauing vſed the aduiſe of ſundry learned and experienced Phyſitians in Norwich) could in any part be mitigated, and ſo extraordinarily vexed thirteene moneths, was conſtrained to go on Crutches, not being able to feed himſelfe, and amended not before this miſchieuous woman was committed to priſon (accuſed for other wickedneſſes of the like kinde) at which time (ſo neere as he could coniecture) he then receiued ſome releaſe of his former paines, though at the preſent when hee made this relation, which was at Candlemas laſt paſt, had not perfectly recouered his wonted ſtrength: for his left hand remained lame, and without vſe.

But thus much by the way onely, omitting how before this accident a great Water-dogge ranne ouer his bed, the doore of the chamber where he lay being ſhut, no ſuch one knowne (for carefull enquiry was made) either to haue been in that houſe where hee lodged, or in the whole Towne at any time.

I doe not inſiſt vpon this, becauſe ſhee did not nominate him or any other vnto vs, but onely thoſe foure already expreſſed: and for the wrongs

 done

done to them, ſhe craued mercy at Gods hands, as for all other her ſins, and in particular for that of Witch-craft, renounced the Diuell, embraced the mercies of God purchaſed by the obedience of Ieſus Chriſt, and profeſſed that her hope was onely by his ſuffering and paſſion to bee ſaued. And all theſe, that is to ſay, her former grieuous offences committed againſt God, and his people, her defiance of the Diuell, and repoſing all confidence of ſaluation in Chriſt Ieſus alone, and his merits, ſhe in particular maner confeſſed openly at the place of execution, in the audience of multitudes of people gathered together (as is vſuall at ſuch times) to be beholders of her death. And made there alſo profeſſion of her faith, and hope of a better life hereafter; and the meanes whereby ſhe truſted to obtaine the ſame, as before, hath beene ſpecified. And being asked, if ſhe would be contented to haue a Pſalme ſung, anſwered willingly that ſhe deſired the ſame, and appointed it herſelfe, *The Lamentation of a Sinner*, whoſe beginning is, *Lord turne not away thy face, &c.* And after the ending thereof thus finiſhed her life: So that in the iudgement of charity we are to conceiue the beſt, and thinke ſhee reſteth in peace, notwithſtanding her heynous tranſgreſſions formerly committed: for there is no maladay incurable to the Almighty Phyſitian, *Eſay* 1. 18. *Ezech.* 33. 11. Therefore *Caine* did iniury to God, when conuicted of the barbarous and vnnaturall murther of his righteous brother, cryed out that his ſinne was greater then could be forgiuen, *Gen.* 4. 13

for

for *Gods* mercy is greater then mans misery can be. And euen for the like vnto this very fact, we haue a booke case, already adiudged, and ouer-ruled in those *Ephesians*, who brought their coniuring bookes, sacrificed them in the fire, æstimated at the[a] value of nine hundred pounds of our money, repented of their[b] sinnes, and obtained mercy, *Acts* 19. *vers*. 19.

[a] *Budæus de asse lib*. 5.

[b] The Ephesians were infamous for their Magicall practises, *Appollonius* professing the same in the Citie, so that it grewe into a prouerb, γράμματα Ἐφέσια, the Ephesian letters, which were certaine Characters and wordes, by vertue whereof they obtained good successe in all businesse, victory against others, euasion and escape from dangers; and as we reade in *Suidas*, a Milesian armed with these letters, ouer-came thirty Champions in the games of *Olimpus*, but being remoued by the Magistrate, hauing intelligence thereof, himselfe was subdued. Of these see *Atheneus Deipnosophiston lib*. 12. *Hesichius* in his *Lexicon*. *Plutarchus quæstionum conuiualium, lib* 7. *cap*. 5.

¶ *The eight Proposition, and first consequent.*

NOw then from this premised narration, these two corrollaries or consequents do necessarily follow.

It is not lawfull for any Christian to consult with a witch or wisard, or goe to them for helpe. God himselfe, whose commandement is and must be the rule of our life & direction hath forbidden it, *Leuit*. 19. 31. and 20. 6. *Deuter*. 18. 10. 11. And the Imperiall lawes, haue beene in this case verie respectiue. [a] Therefore, *Leo* the Emperour

[a] *Cod lib*. 9. *titulo* 18. *L*. *nullus*. & *L*. *Nemo*.

straitly enioyneth, that none should resort vnto them, and stileth their aduice nothing but meere impostures and deceit; and in the [b] Decrees collected by *Gratian*, the teachers of the people are seriously exhorted to admonish them, that magicall arts and inchantments cannot heale any infirmity: and that they bee the dangerous snares, and subtilties of that ancient enemy of mankind, by which he indeuoureth to entangle them [c]: and these so streight and seuere prohibitions are not without iust and weighty cause. For,

[b] *Gratianus decretorum parte 2.caus.26-qu.7.*

[c] *Danaeus in dialogo de sortiariys cap.6.*

First, wee must haue no commerce or dealing with the diuell, eyther directly and immediately, or mediately and indirectly; for we ought to haue our recourse to God alone in all distresses, and this is that which *Eliah* spake with great indignation vnto the messengers of *Ahaziah*, who went to enquire of *Baal-zebub*, for the recouerie of their Lords health, 2.*King*.1.3. [d] So that wee must not seeke to Sathan, or any of his ministers. For none can serue two maisters, *Matt*.6.24. But as religious *Iehosaphat*, when we know not what to doe, then lift vp our eyes to heauen, 2.*Chron*.20.12.

[d] *Martinus de Arles in tractatu de superstitionibus. Iohannes Gerson de erroribus circa artem magicam articulo 5.*

Secondly, that help which any receiue from them bringeth destruction of our soules, for such as seeke for reliefe this way, make a [e] separation &

[e] In curing diseases the diuell respecteth two ends: the one, that he might seeme to keep the promise he hath made with those his slaues, and retaine them in their malicious practises and infidelity: the other, that hee might draw their faith and trust from God, who are thus healed by witches and wisards his instruments, and cast them downe headlong into destruction of their soules: or if they misse of hoped reliefe which often times so commeth to passe, God withstanding their attempts, then to wound their consciences, and driue them to despaire.

departing

departing from God, which is the death of the soule. And though it may be obiected, that some haue receiued benefite hereby, yet these are not one of tenne. And further, wee are not to iudge heerein of the lawfulnesse of these actions by the successe, but rest vpon the commaundement, for it falleth out sometime, that a thiefe and common robber by the high way, may liue in more aboundance, then those who with a lawfull and honest trade painefully maintaine them selues, yet therefore hee is not iustified. And when wee haue recourse vnto others beside God, we bewray herein our [f] distrust, infidelitie, contempt and rebellion against him, which grieuous sinnes bring his wrath and eternall destruction. But let it be taken for granted, that wee may receiue good by them, yet this maxime is sure, & a truth vnrepealeable, which no distinction can elude; we must not doe euill that good may come thereof, *Rom.* 3.8. [g] yea, it were better to end our dayes in any extremitie whatsoeuer, then to vse these for our helpers.

[f] *Nauarrus in Enchiridio siue manuali confessariorum cap* 11

[g] *Chrysost. cont. Iudæos hom.* 6.

Thirdly, they [h] cure not diseases but in shew, except such as themselues haue inflicted, otherwise those doe returne, as is reported of *Adrianus* the [i] Emperour, who troubled with a dropsie, by magicall charmes did oftentimes empty the water thereof, but in a short space increased againe; and perceiuing the same to grow worse & worse, sought to dispatch and rid himselfe of life, by poyson, or the sword, or some other desperate attēpts. Or a worse malady (the first being abated) followeth: as I haue knowne one, who vsing the help of

[h] *Tatianus oratione tertia contra Græcos.*

[i] *Xiphilinus ex Dion. in Adriano* μαγγανείαις μέν τισὶ καὶ γοητείαις ἐξεκένετο ποτὲ τοῦ ὑγροῦ, πάλιν δὲ αὐτοῦ ἐνεπίμπλατο.

a wisard for the cure of a sore in his breast, prescribed in this sort: crossed the place affected with his thumb, and mumbled to himselfe some words in secret, after gaue the patient a powder like the ashes of wood, which was to be boiled in running water, and with it to wash the vlcer, after certaine clouts were to be applyed, with speciall care to lay that side of the clout vnto the sore, which was by him crossed, and marked; and all these clothes must at once be bound vpon it, and euery day the lowest remoued or taken away: thus in short time that anguish and griefe ceased; but not long after the party fell into a more grieuous infirmity, and still continueth therein. Or if the euill be taken from the [k] person presently afflicted, then is it layd vpon his friends children or cattell, and sometime it falleth to the lot of the witch herselfe, so that alwayes the diuell is a diuell, doing euill, and working mischiefe.

[k] Bodine proueth this by many examples in his *Demonomania. lib. 3. cap. 2.*

Fourth, a [l] wisard, witch, or sorcerer can not releeue any but by his or her inuocation, and help of the diuell, but this fact is absolutely, and without exception, wicked, and can by no limitation or circumstance bee made tolerable: Therefore they who require this at their hands, which they cannot performe without committing of sinne, be liable to the same vengeance and wrath of God to which they are; for not only the principall offenders, but the [m] accessaries, and consenters to their euill, are worthy of death, *Rom.* 1. 32.

[l] *Binfeldius de confessionibus malificorum. Cardinalis Caietanus in summula titulo de maleficio. Toletus in summa casuum consciëatiæ, siue instructione sacerdotum li. 4. c. 16.*

[m] *Gratianus in Decretis parte 2. causa 26. quæst. 2. sect. Qui sine saluatore, &c.*

Now before I conclude this poynt, because by these kinde of creatures, many toyes bee vsed, to

shadow

shaddow and maske the diuells suggestion and workes, it shall not be amisse to mention some of them, and among the rest be [n] characters written or grauen in plates of mettall: and for these it is most certayne that Quantities haue no actiue qualitie; and therefore, if any expected successe according to desire doe follow in the vse thereof, it proceedeth from the illusion of Sathan, and is his worke, that hereby he might winne credite to his crafty sleights and conueyances, and procure to himselfe authority, establishing the kingdome of darkenesse, withdraw men from resting vpon God, and reposing their trust in his almighty power, and boundlesse mercy, and sollicite them to expect helpe from him. There are besides these, other idle trifles (for they deserue no better name which are appoynted to be hung about the neck) for Amulets, as [o] powerfull and effectuall remedies against certayne diseases, and pictures made of gold, brasse, lead, wax, &c. which neyther haue nor can haue any other vertue, then that which they doe receiue from the matter wherof they be framed, for the figure worketh not as a cause of alteration; but if it bring to passe any other effect that is from the power of the diuell an old enemy, and craftie deluder of mankinde, and therefore, presupposeth a contract made with him: wherefore [p] *Antoninus Caracalla* condemned those who vsed the same, for the helpe of Tertian and Quartan agues, and *Constantius* [q] decreeth such to be woorthy capitall punishment, and put to death. And that naturall couer wherewith some children

[n] Of these characters and Images, *Iohn Gerson de erroribus circa artē magicam dicto 3. litera O. Martinus de Arles de superstitionibus. Binfeldius in cōmentar. ad titulum Codicis de maleficis et mathematicis*; and examples *Hector Boetius l. 2. historiæ Scoticæ, de rege Duffo*, and *Thuanus* lately in the reign of *Charles* the ninth king of France in the 57. Booke of the historie of his times.

[o] *Binfeldius in titulum codicis de maleficis & mathematicis. Martinus de Arles in tractatu de superstitionibus.*

[p] *Spartianus in vita Antonini Caracallæ.*

[q] *Ammianus Marcellinus lib. 19. non procul a fine, & lib. 29.*

are borne, and is called by our women, the sillie how, Midwiues were wont to sell to credulous Aduocates and Lawyers, as an especiall meanes to furnish them with eloquence [r] and perswasiue speech, and to stoppe the mouthes of all, who should make any opposition against them: for which cause one [s] *Protus* was accused by the Clergie of Constantinople to haue offended in this matter. And *Chrysostome* often accuseth Midwiues for reseruing the same to Magicall vses. And *Clemens* [t] *Alexandrinus* giueth vs to vnderstand of one *Ereccestus*, who had two inchaunted rings, so framed, that by the sound thereof he had direction for the fit time and opoortunity in mannaging all the businesses hee intended, and yet notwithstanding was priuily murthered, though hee had warning giuen by that sound which was his vsuall instructer. Thus, none can escape the reuenging hand of God, which pursueth those who haue infeoffed themselues to such vanities, and are besotted with these vnlawfull curiosities. But among all other, charmes and inchaunting spells, haue gotten the start of the rest, which some think absolutely lawfull, and may vpon warrantise bee vsed, and pleade prescription for their iustification; for wee reade in *Homer* [u] that *Vlysses* being wounded by words, stayed the flux of blood; and [x] *Cardanus* tells vs, that himselfe cutting his lip, could by no meanes restraine the flowing blood, vntill he charmed it, and then presently stanched: but dare not affirm whether his owne confidence, or the words did make this restraint. I might adde

[r] *Lampridius in Antonino Diadumeo.*

[s] *Balsamon in commentarijs ad conc. Constantinopolitanum in Trullo cap. 61.*

[t] *Stromateon libr. 1. gestauit* δύο δακτυλίους γοητευομένους· ἀπέθανε δὲ ὅμως δολοφονηθεὶς καίτοι προσημαίνοντος τοῦ ψόφου.

[u] *Odissea 19. vulnus Vlyssis* Αὐτολύκου φίλοι παῖδες δῆσαν ἐπισταμένως ἐπαοιδῇ δ᾽ αἷμα κελαινὸν ἔσχεθον.
Cato de re rustica.
Plin. li. 28. ca. 2.
Bodinus Dæmonomanias l. 2. c. 2.

[x] *De subtilitate libr. 18.*

to theſe, that infallible meanes (as is ſuppoſed) by finding out a thiefe with a Siue and a payre of Sheares, with that coniunction[y] *Dies, mies, Ieſ-cet, &c.* and the reſt of ſuch ſenceleſſe and monſtrous tearmes, a Riddle that *Oedipus* himſelfe could not vnfolde. But becauſe this conceit of charming hath ouer-ſpread it ſelfe in this Sunne-ſet of the world, and challengeth a lawfull approbation from the authority and practiſe of ancient[z] Phyſitians, yea and found ſome[a] Diuines to be their Patrons reſpectiuely, and with clauſes of mitigation, I thinke it very neceſſarie to ſhew the vnlawfulneſſe thereof. Wherefore,

Firſt, they had their originall and beginning from the diuell, who abode not in the truth, *Iohn* 8.44. was caſt downe with the apoſtata angels to hell, and deliuered into chaines of darkeneſſe, 2. *Pet.*2.4. who enuying mans felicity receiued into grace after the[b] fall, himſelfe eternally reiected, omitted no occaſion to weaken and ouerthrow the ſame, that the benefite thereof might come but to a few, and the greateſt number periſh with him for euer. Whereupon he endeuoured to inwrappe the weaker ſort of that fraile corporation in ſuperſtitions, beguile them with doubtfull and falſe oracles, and bring to a forme of worſhippe contrary to that which God had commaunded, [c] whereby the world beganne to abound with Idolatry, diſobedience, contempt, murthers, vncleaneneſſe, luſts, thefts, lying, and ſuch like outrages: and that hee might with his infections impoyſon them more dangerouſly, and ſoueraigne in

[y] *Georgius Pictorius in epitome de Magia. cap.*21.

[z] *Vide Ritherhuſium in notis ad Malchum de vita Pythagoræ. Alexander Trallian.libr.*10.*de colico affectu, in fine. Serenus Sammonicus de præceptis medicinæ cap.de Hemitritæo depellenda. Ioh.Langius epiſtolarum medicinalium lib.*1 *epiſt.*33.*&* 34.

[a] *Aquinas in ſumma ſecunda ſecundæ queſt.* 96.*articulo* 4.

[b] *De differentia inter Diabolos & homines peccatores Auguſtinus in Enchiridio cap.*28.*& in ſuis ad illum cōmentarijs Lambertus Danæus.*

[c] *Peucerus de generibus Diuinationum & titulo de incantationibus.*

in their hearts, he vndertooke to worke wonders, imitating such miracles as God had done, and deuised cunningly many subtile sleights and legerdemaines, and for this end most blasphemously abused the glorious and holy name of God, and the word vttered by his mouth, and represented a false shew of those effects, which hee had wrought in nature: and heerein leuelled at two intentions, one to reproch God, and countercheeke his works; the other to ouer-mask and couer his owne secret traps and frauds, perswading men, that by the power of wordes these things were brought to passe, which must needes therefore be of great efficacie: seeing that the world & all things therein were so made of nothing; for he spake, and they were created, and thus practised to disgrace, and extenuate, that admirable and great worke of Creation, and cause men to make lighter account of the Creator, seeing that they also (instructed by him) were enabled thorow the pronunciation of certayne words contriued into a speciall forme, eyther to infuse new strength into things, or depriue them of that which formerly they had, or alter the course of Nature, in raysing tempests, stirring vp thunder and lightning; in [d] taming serpents, and depriuing them of their naturall fiercenesse and venime, and cause wilde beasts to become meeke and tractable, yea in seeming to make sensible bodies; as cloudes, wind, raine & the like. And thus the diuell is that father who begot Charmes, and brought them foorth, not powerfull in themselues, but by that

[d] *Frigidus in pratis cantando rumpitur anguis* Virg. ecloga 8.

inter-

inter-league which hee hath with those who are invassaled vnto him.

Secondly, God doth as straitly prohibit them, and seuerely punish the practisers thereof, as others offending in any exercise of vnlawfull arts, *Deut*. 18. 10. 11. There shall not be found among you (instructing the Israelites his people) a charmer, &c. for these are abhomination vnto the Lord, &c. And this is recorded in the Catalogue of those sinnes of *Manasses*, by which hee sought to prouoke God vnto anger, 2. *Kin*. 21.8. 2. *Chronicles* 33.6.

Thirdly, words haue no vertue,[e] but either to signifie and expresse the conceits of the minde, or to affect the eares of the Auditors, so that they can worke nothing but in these two respects: first of the matter which is vttered by them, which vnderstood of the hearers, affect the mind diuersly, and that especially when there is ioyned with it a comelinesse of action and pronunciation, as wee we see oftentimes in the speeches of the Ministers of the Word, and in the pleadings of Orators. As when *Paul* reasoned before *Fœlix* and *Drusilla* his wife, of Temperance, Righteousnesse, and Iudgement to come, hee trembled, *Acts* 24. 25. [f] being guilty to himselfe of fraudulent and cruell dealing, of lasciuiousnesse and a filthy life, and therefore might iustly feare vengeance for the same.

A like example to this is that in King *Agrippa*, though working vpon a better subiect, *Act*. 26. 28. And if I may conioyne Diuine eloquence

[e] ῥήματα τὰ Ελασημ-ματα τονηματων, & φωνὴ *Etymologicis dicitur quasi* τὸ φῶς τοῦ νοῦ. *De hac materia eruditissimè disputat Franciscus Valesius de sacra Philosophia, cap.* 3.

[f] *Præfectus Iudeæ impositus cuncta malefacta sibi impunè ratus est, &c. Tacitus Annalium lib.* 12. *& historiæ lib.* 5. *per omnem sæuitiam ac libidinem ius regium seruili ingenio exercuit*

with Humane, it is memorable, that while[g] *Tully* pleaded before *Cæsar* for *Ligarius*, accused by *Tubero*, to haue beene confederate with *Pompey*, purposing to put him to death, as an enemy, when the Orator altered, and in Rhetoricall manner inforced his speech, the other changed accordingly his countenance, and bewrayed the piercing words to be so affecting, that the supplications, when he came once to vrge and mention the battell of *Pharsalia*, (trembling and dismayed) did fall from his hands, hauing the passions of his minde extraordinarily moued, and absolued the offender. Or else when by their pleasantnesse, with delight they slide into the hearts of men, and rauish their affections: and thus it was with[h] *Augustine*, as he acknowledgeth of himselfe, that being at *Milaine* where he was baptized by S. *Ambrose*, when he heard the harmony which was in singing of the Psalmes, the words pierced his eares, the truth melted his heart, his passions were moued, and showers of teares with delight fell from his eyes.[i] But these effects are wrought onely in such who vnderstand that which is spoken, but neither of both these properties are to bee found in the Charmes of Wisards: besides, that they are conceiued and expressed in monstrous and vnknowne tearmes, not intelligible, and without signification: and therefore the effects they produce being[k] supernaturall must proceed from that secret compact, at the least made with the Diuell.

Fourthly, these charmes are meere mockeries, and

[g] ἀρξάμενε λέγειν ὁ κικέρων ὑπερφυῶς ἐκίνει. *Plutarchus in Cicerone.*

[h] *Aug. confessionum lib. 9. cap. 6 Quantum fleui in hymnis & cãtibus eius suauè sonãtibus Ecclesiæ tuæ vocibus commotus acriter? Voces illę influebant auribus meis, & liquebatur veritas tua in cor meum, & ex ea æstuabat affectus pietatis, & currebant lachrimæ & bene mihi erat cum ijs.*

[i] *Vide Aquinatem egregie de hac materia disputantẽ Summa contra Gentes, lib. 43. cap. 105. & tuis Commentatorem Franciscum de Syluestris.*

[k] *Caietanus in summula in titulo: Incantatio. Toletus in summa causuum conscientiæ, siue instructione sacerdotum lib. 4. cap. 17.*

and grosse abuses, both of God, and Men his creatures, I will giue you a taste of one or two, whereby you may iudge of the rest, for they came all out of one shoppe, and are fashioned in one forge, and haue the same workman or Artificer. [l] An old woman crauing helpe for bleare eyes, had deliuered a Billet of Paper to weare about her necke, in which was written, *The Diuell pull out thine eyes*, and recouered. Another tied a scroule to a sicke man, full of strange Characters, with which were intermingled a few names of Diuels, as *Lucifer*, *Sathan*, *Belzebub*, *Oriens*, *Behal*, *Mammon*, *Beuflar*, *Narthin Oleasar*, *&c.* and other of this sort; but what manner of blessing this was, and how likely to be medicinable, a Christian truely instructed in Gods word knoweth; and the Lord who is the father of mercies, and God of all comfort, preserue vs from such blasphemies, which are the Diuels Sacrifices.

[l] *Godelmannus in tractatu de magis, Veneficis &c. lib.* 1. *cap.* 8 *no* 26 *&* 27. *vide Simonem Maiolum colloquiorum siue dierum caniculorum parte* 2, *colloquio* 3.

Fifthly, the discreeter sort among the Heathen, by that small glimpse of naturall reason which they had, misliked of these things: [m] And therefore *Cato* among the rest of admonitions to the Bailiffe of his husbandry, giueth this charge, to aske no aduice of any Southsaier, Diuiner, Wisard, or Natiuity Calculator. [n] And *Columella* vtterly forbiddeth all acquaintance with Witches, wherby ignorant people are inforced to expence in detestable Arts, and mischieuous deeds. [o] *Hippocrates* doth almost like a Christian discourse of this poynt, and condemne the whole practise of this Art, as iniurions vnto God, who onely purgeth

[m] *Cato de re rustica, cap.* 5.

[n] *Columella lib.* 1. *cap.* 8.

[o] *Libro de morbo sacro (siue illius sit, siue alterius, nam de authore apud eruditos dubitatio est) statim ab initio. & quædã huc pertinentia habet Theophrastus de plantis lib.* 9. *cap.* 21.

geth sinnes, and is our preseruer; and for these fellowes who make profession of such wonder-working, brandeth them for Impostors and deceiuers. I conclude with that remarkeable saying of an ancient Diuine; [p] These vanities doe separate and with-draw vs from God, though they may seeme to haue something in them to allure and delight vs; yet let no Christian entertaine them, whose hope ought to be setled in God alone. And if thou be in distresse, or afflicted with sicknesse of body, and feele no present release or comfort, what then? here is the tryall of thy patience, haue not recourse to superstitious and vnlawfull helpers, although they promise thee present remedy; and when they fore-tell thee of things which doe truely according to the prediction so fall out, beleeue them not, follow the example of Christ, who rebuked the Diuell, though he called him (as he was indeed) the Son of God. For vnder the vaile of truth he shadoweth falshood; euen as if one should sweeten with honey or sugar the brimme of the Cup wherein he bringeth poyson: But some will say, they call vpon the name of the Lord of Sabbaoth. Well, but this title they giue not to God, but to the Diuell: therefore betake thou thy selfe to God alone, craue health at his hand, and follow the Apostles direction; *If any bee sicke among you, let him call for the Elders of the Church, and let him pray,* Iames 5. 14.

[p] *Procopius Gazeus in Leuiticum.*

The

The ninth Proposition, and second Corrolary.

THere hath alwayes beene ſome wanton, or peruerſe wits, who only to make triall of their skill, would take in hand to defend abſurd poſitions, and commend both ſuch things and perſons, which were infamous, and contemptible as [q] *Phauorinus* writ the praiſe of the Quartane Ague, one of the gout, blindneſſe, and deafneſſe: [r] *Lucian* of a flye, [ſ] *Eraſmus* of folly, [t] *Syneſius* of baldneſſe, [u] *Glaucus* in *Plato* of iniuſtice. And among the exerciſes of the [x] ancient Orators, wee finde thoſe who ſtrained all their vnderſtanding to blaze the honour of that witleſſe and deformed Coward *Therſites*. And this they haue performed with great Art and eloquence, onely to ſhew their faculty, but neuer in good earneſt took ſuch a matter in hand And therefore more deeply is hee to be cenſured, who hath made himſelfe an aduocate to plead the cauſe of [y] Witches, and defend thẽ as innocent. And becauſe this is a dangerous example, and doth draw thoſe who are euill affected to offend, hoping for patronage of their impiety, I adde for concluſion this laſt propoſition: Wiſards, Witches, and the whole rabble of Sorcerers (no kinde excepted) are iuſtly liable [z] to extreame puniſhment. The arguments alleaged for proofe

[q] *Phauorinus apud Agellium. lib.17.cap.12.*
[r] *Luciani encomion muscę.*
[ſ] *Eraſmus.*
[t] *Syneſius.*
[u] *Lib. 2. de Republica.*
[x] *Extat eius laudatio inter exempla exercitationum Rhetorum ab Henrico Stephano editarum cum Polemonis & Himerij declamationibus.*
[y] *Wierus.*
[z] *Simlerus in 22 Exodi.*

proofe hereof, are many: I will make choyce of a few (with reference to such authors in whose writings more may bee found) and those which are most [a] demonstratiue.

First, God himselfe hath enacted that pœnall statute, *Thou shalt not suffer a Witch to liue*. *Exod.* 22 18. and nameth here a [b] woman practising this damnable Art for two reasons: First, they are more inclinable hereunto then man. Secondly, that though their fault may seeme, as being the weaker, excuseable, and is in this respect extenuated by some, yet is not therefore to bee spared, whether of that sort which they call [c] good, or bad (for so are they distinguished) & there be some who neuer brought [d] harme vpon any in body, goods, or minde. The cause of this so sharpe a doome, is their compacting with the Diuell, openly or secretly, whereby they couenant to vse his helpe, in fulfilling their desires, and by this meanes make themselues guilty of horrible impiety: for in this they renounce the Lord, who hath created them; make no account of his fauour and protection, cut themselues off from the couenant made with him in baptisme, from the communion of Saints, the true fellowship and seruice of God; and on the contrary yeeld themselues by this confederacy, to Sathan, as their God (and therefore nothing more frequent and vsuall in their mouthes, then my God will do this and that for me) him they continually feare and honour. And thus do at the last become professed enemies both to God and Man. You may adde to this former

[a] Of these all the following reasons. *Binfeldius de confessionibus maleficorum, & in Commentaryis ad titulum legis de maleficis & mathematicis copiosè. Remigius de Dæmonologia, lib.3.cap.vltimo. Peucerus de præcipuis Diuinationum generibus. Erastus de Lamyis. Bodinus Dæmonomanias, lib.4.cap.5.*

[b] *Hironimus Oleaster in locum, & Iunius & Tremelius in eundem.*

[c] Perkins of Witch-craft.

[d] *Binfeldius in Commentarium ad titulum Codicis de Mathematicis & Maleficis.*

ther law, that which is *Leuit.* 19. 26. *& cap.*6. *You shall vse no inchantment : the soule that turneth after such as haue familiar spirits, and are Wisards, to goe a whooring after them, I will set my face against that soule, and will cut him off from among his people, &c.* Againe, *Deut.*18.10. *There shall not bee found among you any that vseth Diuination, nor an obseruer of times, or an inchanter, or a Witch, or a Charmer, or a consulter with familiar spirits, a Wisard, or Necromancer.* And that God might shew how[e] much *Manasses* had prouoked him to wrath, through his transcendent and outragious sinnes in the Catalogue thereof, his conspiring with Diuels is mentioned 1.*King*.21.8. And therefore is depriued of his kingdome, bound in fetters, and carried captiue vnto *Babel*, 2. *Chron.* 33. 6. 11. and though he repented of these outragious and enormious transgressions, yet God would not bee appeased for them fiftie yeares after he was dead, *Ierem.*15.4.

Secondly, the ciuill lawes in this case are most strict, decreeing them to bee burned, and their goods confiscate, though they were persons of quality, and honourable, seated in dignity, and place of authority: and there is a seuere constitution made by *Charles* the fift in late dayes against them, that though they shall not haue done, or be conuinced to haue hurt any, yet because they attempted a thing vnlawfull, and abhominable vnto God, are extraordinarily to be punished. And concerning this particular, S. *Augustin* discourseth excellently, worthy to be read, *de ciu. dei. l.*8.*c.*19.

e *Gode lmannus de Magis & veneficis, l. b.*3.*cap.*11.*no.*14.15.16.*& seq.*

f *Anonymus de Mosaicarum & Romanarum legum collatione titulo.*15.

g *Constitutiones criminales Caroli* 5[i]. *à Georgio Ramo edita cap.* 44.109.& 177. Such are exempted from all benefit of those pardons which Princes vse to giue to other malefactors. *Fornerius ad legem* 236. *in Titulo de verborum significatione, vide illum nam multa erudite scribit, ad propositum nostrum pertinentia.*

Thirdly, God willeth those should bee put to death, who by Diabolicall and vnlawfull Arts, do endeuour to helpe or harme others, whether in act they performe the same, or purpose with intention, conceiuing and thinking they can do it, with ranke Witches must needes be marshalled; and therefore iustly subiect to deserued punishment.

Fourthly, all Idolaters are to dye by diuine appointment, *Deu.* 17. 5. But I thinke no mans forehead is so brasen, that will stand Proctor, and plead guiltlesse for these sort of people, who deuote themselues wholly to the Diuell, though neuer so closely, and with great and cautelous secresie: and no doubt God therefore was reuenged of the Templars, and their detestable wickednesse practised in darknesse and obscurity, who all [h] perished, as it were, in a moment for the same; of which at the full we may be informed in our owne ancient histories.

[h] *Anno Domini* 1312. whose order began 1123. *Thomas Walsingham* in the life of K. *Edward* the 2d, in his English history, and in his *Hypodigma Neustrie.*

Fifthly, they doe solicite others to be of their profession (which is one clause of that contract made betweene them and the Diuell) and consecrate their children vnto him: and against this, there is an especiall caution put in *Deteronomy* 13. 6. 9. 10.

Sixtly, they deserue death as inhumane and barbarous tyrants, for lingringly *vt sentiant se mori*, that they may feele how they doe decay by degrees, seek the vtter ouerthrow of those whom they doe maligne: and as a further appendix to this, oftentimes by the helpe of their grand teacher,

cher, sowe discord betweene husband and wife, sollicite maydens, yea enforce both them, and married women to vncleane, and vnlawfull lusts, and heerein implore the helpe of the diuell, to accomplish their malicious designes, which transgression is capitall.

Seuenthly, the exercise of this act or vanity is punishable by death, although it be practised but onely in sport and ieast, which may appeare thus, because God hath seriously forbidden (and vnder no lesse forfeiture then of life it self) to aske counsell of a Soothsayer or Coniurer; if this then be a crime of such nature, in those, who it may bee heerein thought not to doe euill, there is no reason to induce any to thinke that hee will spare the wilfull, and purposed authors thereof, and Magitians, who worke onely iuggling trickes, and illusions, and fore-tell some future things, as yet vnknowne vntill they doe so fall out, are not freed from the sentence condemnatorie; much more then those who willingly, and vpon premeditated malice, murther or impaire the life and good estate of other, deserue to stand parallell with them. And there can no reson be yielded of this so sharp a censure, but onely because they haue learned, and accordingly exercise vnlawfull arts, for whosoeuer endeuoureth to bring that thing to passe, by pretending naturall meanes, which exceedeth the power of Nature, and is not thereunto enabled eyther by God, or the ministery of good Angells at his appoyntment, hee must of necessity haue this faculty communicated by some combination and inter league with the diuell.

Eightly, the Iudge or ciuil Magistrate is bound by vertue of that office, and superioritie he sustaineth in the common-wealth, to purge and free that place, in, and ouer which he hath command, of all malefactors, which if he doe neglect, then is a double offender, against the Law both of Iustice and Charity; for hee is obliged by duety to foresee (so much as in him lyeth) that the publike state should be secured, which it concerneth to haue offenders punished, otherwise hee maketh himselfe partner with them in their outrages and offences, and standeth answerable for those dammages sustained by the whole bodie of the people in generall, or vndergone by any particular of the same, for sparing of the wicked [i] is hurting the good, and hee that doth not represse and forbid euill (when it is in his power) doth countenance and maintaine it.

[i] *Pythagoras apud Stobæum.*

Much more might be added, and many examples produced, to manifest, how in all Nations these odious company of witches, and the like haue euer beene accounted detestable; and for their impious deedes requited with neuer dying shame, and vtter confusion, and iustly by law executed; for among the Romans, Mathematitians, [k] and Magitians by the Decree of the Senate were expelled out of all Italy: and amongst these *Pituanus* was throwne downe from the rock *Tarpeius*, and crushed apeeces. *Martius* by the Consuls put to death with the sound of a Trumpet without the gate *Exquilina*: *Publicia* and *Licinia*

[k] *Tacitus annalium li.2. et consule Lipsium in suis ad eum cōmentarijs.*

tinia [l] women, and seauenty more witches hanged. The [m] speedy iudgement of the Athenians, witnesse of their hatred against these kinde of malefactors, is much commended, who without any other solemnity of proceeding at the onely accusation of a Maide, without delay put one *Lemnia* a witch to death: and it is memorable which *Ammianus* [n] *Marcellinus* hath left in record, that one *Hilarius*, because hee committed his sonne yong, and not of mature yeares, to be taught and instructed vnto a Coniurer, was adiudged to die, and escaping from the hands of the executioner, who had negligently bound him, drawne by force out of the next church of the Christians, to which hee fled as vnto a Sanctuary, and executed.

[l] *Valerius Maximus li. 6. ca 3. Remigius Demonolog. l. 3. c. m.*
[m] *Demosthenes orat. 1. contra Aristogitonem.*
[n] *Libr. 26.* not farre from the beginning.

The end of [o] *Varasolo*, a famous Inchantresse in Hungarie is dreadfull, who for her sundry witcheries was cast into prison, and there constrayned through extremity of hunger, to teare off and eate the flesh of her owne legges and armes, and at the last, impatient of further delay, there murthered herselfe, and shortned the span of her life.

[o] *Bonfinius rerum Hungaricarum decadis 2. libr. 2.*

But here I stay my hand, take it from the table, and the rather, because much hath already beene spoken to this purpose. Wherefore, for conclusion, I shut vp this whole Treatise with a remarkeable speech of a noble [p] King; Let the streight ri-

[p] *Allaricus apud Cassiodorum li. 9. epist. 18. in qua edictum illius*; and *Cornelius Agrippa*, sometime more then well acquainted with this Art, doth retract his owne books written of secret philosophy, & in plaine tearms and expresly giues his iudgement, that all these lewd women (for this title may include the whole rabble of this blacke Guard) with *Iannes* and *Iambres*, and *Simon Magus*, are to be tormented with endlesse paines in eternall fire. *Cornelius Agrippa De vanitate Scientiarum ca. 48.*

gour:

gor of law bee inflicted vpon all, both practisers and partakers with wisards, by putting any confidence in them; for it is vngodly for man to be remisse and fauourable vnto those whom diuine piety, and our duety to God will not suffer vnpunished. For what folly were it to forsake the Creator and Giuer of life, and to follow the author of death? this dishonest fact, vnbeseeming, and vtterly repugnant to the credite and reputation of a Iudge, be farre from him. Let none countenance that which the Lawes doe condemne, for all are by the Regall Edicts to bee punished with death, who intermeddle with such forbidden and vnlawfull Artes.

FINIS.

Matthew Hopkins Witch Finder Generall
My Imps names are
Holt.
1 Ilemauzar
2 Pyewackett
Jarmara
Sacke & Sugar
3 Pecke in the Crowne
4 Griezzell Greedigutt
Newes
Vinegar tom

THE Discovery of Witches:

IN

Answer to severall QUERIES,

LATELY

Delivered to the Judges of Assize for the County of NORFOLK.

And now published

By MATTHEW HOPKINS, Witch-finder.

FOR

The Benefit of the whole KINGDOME.

EXOD. 22. 18.

Thou shalt not suffer a witch to live.

LONDON,

Printed for *R. Royston*, at the Angell in Ivie Lane.

M. DC. XLVII.

Certaine *Queries* answered, which have been and are likely to be objected against MATTHEW HOPKINS, in his way of finding out *Witches*.

QUERIE I.

THat he must needs be the greatest Witch, Sorcerer, and Wizzard himselfe, else hee could not doe it.

Answ. If *Satans* kingdome be divided against it selfe, how shall it stand?

Querie 2. *If he never went so farre as is before mentioned, yet for certaine he met with the Devill, and cheated him of his Booke, wherein were written all the Witches names in* England, *and if he looks on any Witch, he can tell by her countenance what she is; so by this, his helpe is from the Devill.*

Answ. If he had been too hard for the devill and got his book, it had been to his great commendation, and no disgrace at all: and for judgement in *Phisiognomie*, he hath no more then any m an else whatsoever.

Quer. 3. *From whence then proceeded this his skill? was it from his profound learning, or from much reading of learned Authors concerning that subiect?*

Answ. From neither of both, but from experience, which though it be meanly esteemed of, yet the surest and safest way to judge by.

Quer. 4. *I pray where was this experience gained? and why gained by him and not by others?*

Answ. The Discoverer never travelled far for it, but in *March* 1644 he had some seven or eight of that horrible sect of Witches living in the Towne where he lived, a Towne in *Essex* called *Maningtree*, with divers other adjacent Witches of other towns, who every six weeks in the night (being alwayes on the Friday night) had their meeting close by his house, and had their severall solemne sacrifices there offered to the *Devill*, one of which this discoverer heard speaking to her *Imps* one night, and bid them goe to another Witch, who was thereupon apprehended, and searched by women who had for many yeares knowne the Devills marks, and found to have three teats about her, which honest women have not: so upon command from the *Justice*, they were to keep her from sleep two or three nights, expecting in that time to see her *familiars*, which the fourth night she called in by their severall names, and told them what shapes, a quarter of an houre before they came in, there being ten of us in the roome, the first she called was

1. *Holt*, who came in like a white kitling.

2. *Jarmara*, who came in like a fat Spaniel without any legs at all, she said she kept him fat, for she clapt her hand on her belly, and said he suckt good blood from her body.

3. *Vinegar Tom*, who was like a long-legg'd Greyhound, with an head like an Oxe, with a long taile and broad eyes, who when this discoverer spoke to, and bade him goe to the place provided for him and his Angels, immediately transformed himselfe into the shape of a child of foure yeeres old without a head, and gave halfe a dozen turnes about the house, and vanished at the doore.

4. *Sack and Sugar*, like a black Rabbet.

5. Newes, like a Polcat. All these vanished away in a little time. Immediately after this Witch confessed severall other Witches, from whom she had her *Imps*, and named to divers women where their marks were, the number of their *Marks*, and *Imps*, and *Imps* names, as *Elemanzer*, *Pyewacket*, *Peckin the Crown*, *Grizzel Greedigut*, *&c.* which no mortall could invent; and upon their searches the same Markes were found, the same number, and in the same place, and the like confessions from them of the same Imps, (though they knew not that we were told before) and so

peached

peached one another thereabouts that joyned together in the like damnable practiſe, that in our Hundred in *Eſſex*, 29. were condemned at once, 4. brought 25. Miles to be hanged, where this Diſcoverer lives, for ſending the Devill li[illegible] Beare to kill him in his garden, ſo by ſeeing diverſe of the [illegible] Papps, and trying wayes with hundreds of them, he gained this experience, and for ought he knowes any man elſe may find them as well as he and his company, if they had the ſame skill and experience.

Quer. 5. *Many poore People are condemned for having a Pap, or Teat about them, whereas many People (eſpecially antient People) are, and have been a long time troubled with naturall wretts on ſeverall parts of their bodies, and other naturall excreſſencies, as Hemerodes, Piles, Childbearing, &c. and theſe ſhall be judged only by one man alone, and a woman, and ſo accuſed or acquitted.*

Anſw, The parties ſo judging can juſtifie their skill to any, and ſhew good reaſons why ſuch markes are not meerly naturall, neither that they can happen by any ſuch naturall cauſe as is before expreſsed, and for further anſwer for their private judgements alone, it is moſt falſe and untrue, for never was any man tryed by ſearch of his body, but commonly a dozen of the ableſt men in the pariſh or elſe where, were preſent, and moſt commonly as many ancient skilfull matrons and midwives preſent when the women are tryed, which marks not only he, and his company atteſt to be very ſuſpitious, but all beholders, the skilfulleſt of them, doe not approve of them, but likewiſe aſsent that ſuch tokens cannot in their judgements proceed from any the above mentioned Cauſes.

Quer. 6. *It is a thing impoſſible for any man or woman to judge rightly on ſuch marks, they are ſo neare to naturall excreſſencies, and they that finde them, durſt not preſently give Oath they were drawne by evill ſpirits, till they have uſed unlawfull courſes of torture to make them ſay any thing for eaſe and quiet, as who would not do? but I would know the reaſons he ſpeakes of, how, and whereby to diſcover the one from the other, and ſo be ſatisfied in that.*

Anſw. The reaſons in breefe are three, which for the preſent he judgeth to differ from naturall marks; which are, 1. He judgeth by the unuſualnes of the place where he findeth the teats in or on

their

their bodies, being farre distant from any usuall place, from whence such naturall markes proceed, as if a witch plead the markes found are Emerods, if I finde them on the bottome of the back-bone, shall I assent with him, knowing they are not neere that veine, and so others by child-bearing, when it may be they are in the contrary part?

2. They are most commonly insensible, and feele neither pin, needle, aule, &c. thrust through them.

3. The often variations and mutations of these marks into severall formes, confirmes the matter; as if a Witch hear a month or two before that the *Witch-finder* (as they call him) is comming, they will, and have put out their Imps to others to suckle them, even to their owne young and tender children; these upon search are found to have dry skinnes and filmes only, and be close to the flesh, keepe her 24. houres with a diligent eye, that none of her Spirits come in any visible shape to suck her; the women have seen the next day after her Teats extended out to their former filling length, full of corruption ready to burst, and leaving her alone then one quarter of an houre, and let the women go up againe, and shee will have them drawn by her Imps close againe: *Probatum est*. Now for answer to their tortures in its due place.

Quer. 7. *How can it possibly be that the Devill being a spirit, and wants no nutriment or sustentation, should desire to suck any blood? and indeed as he is a Spirit he cannot draw any such excressences, having neither flesh nor bone, nor can be felt, &c.*

Ans. He seekes not their bloud, as if he could not subsist without that nourishment, but he often repairs to them, and gets it, the more to aggravate the Witches damnation, and to put her in mind of her *Covenant*: and as he is a Spirit and Prince of the ayre, he appeares to them in any shape whatsoever, which shape is occasioned by him through joyning of condensed thickned aire together, and many times doth asume shapes of many creatures; but to create any thing he cannot do it, it is only proper to God: But in this case of drawing out of these Teats, he doth really enter into the body, reall, corporeall, substantiall creature, and forceth that Creature (he working in it) to his desired ends, and useth the organs of that body to speake withall to make his compact

pact up with the Witches, be the creature Cat, Rat, Mouse, &c.

Quer. 8. *When these Paps are fully discovered, yet that will not serve sufficiently to convict them, but they must be tortured and kept from sleep two or three nights, to distract them, and make them say any thing; which is a way to tame a wilde Colt, or Hawke, &c.*

Ans. In the infancy of this discovery it was not only thought fitting, but enjoyned in *Essex* and *Suffolke* by the Magistrates, with this intention only, because they being kept awake would be more the active to cal their Imps in open view the sooner to their helpe, which oftentimes have so happened; and never or seldome did any Witch ever complaine in the time of their keeping for want of rest, but after they had beat their heads together in the Goale; and after this use was not allowed of by the Judges and other Magistrates, it was never since used, which is a yeare and a halfe since, neither were any kept from sleep by any order or direction since; but peradventure their own stubborne wills did not let them sleep, though tendered and offered to them.

Quer. 9. *Beside that unreasonable watching, they were extraordinarily walked, till their feet were blistered, and so forced through that cruelty to confesse, &c.*

Ans. It was in the same beginning of this discovery, and the meaning of walking of them at the highest extent of cruelty, was only they to walke about themselves the night theywere watched, only to keepe them waking: and the reason was this, when they did lye or sit in a chaire, if they did offer to couch downe, then the watchers were only to desire them to sit up and walke about, for indeed when they be suffered so to couch, immediately comes their Familiars into the room and scareth the watchers, and hearteneth on the Witch, though contrary to the true meaning of the same instructions, diverse have been by rusticall People, (they hearing them confess to be Witches) mis-used, spoiled, and abused, diverse whereof have suffered for the same, but could never be proved against this Discoverer to have a hand in it, or consent to it; and hath likewise been un-used by him and others, ever since the time they were kept from sleepe.

Quer. 10. *But there hath been an abominable, inhumane, and un-*

mercifull tryall of these poore creatures, by tying them, and heaving them into the water; a tryall not allowable by Law or conscience, and I would faine know the reasons for that.

Ans. It is not denyed but many were so served as had Papps, and floated, others that had none were tryed with them and sunk, but marke the reasons.

For first the Divels policie is great, in perswading many to come of their owne accord to be tryed, perswading them their marks are so close they shall not be found out, so as diverse have come 10. or 12. Miles to be searched of their own accord, and hanged for their labour, (as one *Meggs* a Baker did, who lived within 7. Miles of *Norwich*, and was hanged at *Norwich* Assizes for witchcraft) then when they find that the Devil tells them false they reflect on him, and he (as 40. have confessed) adviseth them to be swome, and tels them they shall sinke and be cleared that way, then when they be tryed that way and floate, they see the Devill deceives them againe, and have so laid open his treacheries.

2. It was never brought in against any of them at their tryals as any evidence.

3. King *James* in his *Demonology* saith, it is a certaine rule, for (saith he). Witches deny their baptisme when they Covenant with the Devill, water being the sole element thereof, and therefore saith he, when they be heaved into the water, the water refuseth to receive them into her bosome, (they being such Miscreants to deny their baptisme) and suffers them to float, as the Froath on the Sea, which the water will not receive, but casts it up and downe, till it comes to the earthy element the shore, and there leaves it to consume.

4. Observe these generation of Witches, if they be at any time abused by being called Whore, Theefe, &c, by any where they live, they are the readiest to cry and wring their hands, and shed tears in abundance, & run with full and right sorrowfull acclamations to some Justice of the Peace, and with many teares make their complaints: but now behold their stupidity; nature or the elements reflection from them, when they are accused for this horible and damnable sin of Witchcraft, they never alter or change

their

their countenances, nor let one Teare fall. This by the way, swimming (by able Divines whom I reverence) is condemned for no way, and therefore of late hath, and for ever shall be left.

Quer. 11. *Oh! but if this torturing Witch-catcher can by all or any of these meanes wring out a word or two of confession from any of these stupified, ignorant, unitelligible, poore silly creatures, (though none heare it but himselfe) he will adde and put her in feare to confesse telling her, else she shall be hanged; but if she doe, he will set her at liberty, and so put a word into her mouth, and make such a silly creature confesse she knowes not what.*

Answ. He is of a better conscience, and for your better understanding of him, he doth thus uncase himselfe to all, and declares what confessions (though made by a Witch against her selfe) he allowes not of, and doth altogether account of no validity, or worthy of credence to be given to it, and ever did so account it, and ever likewise shall.

1. He utterly denyes that confession of a Witch to be of any validity, when it is drawn from her by any torture or violence whatsoever; although after watching, walking, or swimming, diverse have suffered, yet peradventure Magistrates with much care and diligence did solely and fully examine them after sleepe, and consideration sufficient.

2. He utterly denyes that confession of a Witch, which is drawn from her by flattery, viz. *if you will confesse you shall go home, you shall not go to the Goale, nor be hanged, &c.*

3. He utterly denyes that confession of a With, when she confesseth any improbability, impossibility, as *flying in the ayre, riding on a broom, &c.*

4. He utterly denyes a confession of a Witch, when it is interrogated to her, and words put into her mouth, to be of any force or effect: as to say to a silly (yet Witch wicked enough) *you have foure Imps, have you not?* She answers affirmatively, Yes: *did they not suck you?* Yes, saith she: *Are not their names so, and so?* Yes, saith shee: *Did not you send such an Impe to kill my child?* Yes saith she, this being all her confession after this manner, it is by him accompted nothing, and he earnestly doth desire that all Magistrates and Jurors would a little more then ever they did, exa-

mine witnesses, about the interrogated confessions.

Quer. 12. *If all these confessions be denyed, I wonder what he will make a confession, for sure it is, all these wayes have been used and took for good confessions, and many have suffered for them, and I know not what, he will then make a confession.*

Answ. Yes, in brief he will declare what confession of a Witch is of validity and force in his judgement, to hang a Witch: when a Witch is first found with teats, then sequestred from her house, which is onely to keep her old associates from her, and so by good counsell brought into a sad condition, by understanding of the horribleness of her sin, and the judgements threatned against her; and knowing the Devils malice and subtile circumventions, is brought to remorse and sorrow for complying with Satan so long, and disobeying Gods sacred Commands, doth then desire to unfold her mind with much bitterness, and then without any of the before-mentioned hard usages or questions put to her, doth of her owne accord declare what was the occasion of the Devils appearing to her, whether ignorance, pride, anger, malice, &c. was predominant over her, she doth then declare what speech they had, what likeness he was in, what voice he had, what familiars he sent her, what number of spirits, what names they had, what shape they were in, what imployment she set them about to severall persons in severall places, (unknowne to the hearers) all which mischiefes being proved to be done, at the same time she confessed to the same parties for the same cause, and all effected, is testimony enough against her for all her denyall.

Quest. 13. *How can any possibly beleeve that the Devill and the Witch joyning together, should have such power, as the Witches confesse, tc kill such and such a man, child, horse, cow, or the like; if we beleeve they can doe what they will, then we derogate from Gods power, who for certaine limits the Devill and the Witch; and I cannot beleeve they have any power at all.*

Answ. God suffers the Devill many times to doe much hurt, and the devill doth play many times the deluder and impostor with these Witches, in perswading them that they are the cause of such and such a murder wrought by him with their consents, when and indeed neither he nor they had any hand in it, as thus:

We

We must needs argue, he is of a long standing, above 6000. yeers, then he must needs be the best Scholar in all knowledges of arts and tongues, & so have the best skill in *Physicke*, judgment in *Physiognomie*, and knowledge of what disease is reigning or predominant in this or that mans body, (and so for cattell too) by reason of his long experience. This subtile tempter knowing such a man lyable to some sudden disease, (as by experience I have found) as *Plurisie*, *Imposthume*, &c. he resorts to divers Witches; if they know the man, and seek to make a difference between the Witches and the party, it may be by telling them he hath threatned to have them very shortly searched, and so hanged for Witches, then they all consult with *Satan* to save themselves, and *Satan* stands ready prepared, with a *What will you have me doe for you, my deare and nearest children, covenanted and compacted with me in my hellish league, and sealed with your blood, my delicate firebrand-darlings.* *The Divells speech to the Witches.* Oh thou (say they) that at the first didst promise to save us thy servants from any of our deadly enemies discovery, and didst promise to avenge and slay all those, we pleased, that did offend us; Murther that wretch suddenly who threatens the down-fall of your loyall subjects. He then promiseth to effect it. Next newes is heard the partie is dead, he comes to the witch, and gets a world of reverence, credence and respect for his power and activeness, when and indeed the disease kills the party, not the Witch, nor the Devill, (onely the Devill knew that such a disease was predominant) and the witch aggravates her damnation by her familiarity and consent to the Devill, and so comes likewise in compass of the Lawes. This is Satans usuall impostring and deluding, but not his constant course of proceeding, for he and the witch doe mischiefe too much. But I would that Magistrates and Jurats would a little examine witnesses when they heare witches confess such and such a murder, whether the party had not long time before, or at the time when the witch grew suspected, some disease or other predominant, which might cause that issue or effect of death.

Quer. 14. *All that the Witch-finder doth, is to fleece the country of their money, and therefore rides and goes to townes to have imployment, and promiseth them faire promises, and it may be doth nothing*

thing for it, and possesseth many men that they have so many wizzards and so many witches in their towne, and so hartens them on to entertaine him.

Ans. You doe him a great deale of wrong in every of these particulars. For, first,

1. He never went to any towne or place, but they rode, writ, or sent often for him, and were (for ought he knew) glad of him.

2. He is a man that doth disclaime that ever he detected a witch, or said, Thou art a witch; only after her tryall by search, and their owne confessions, he as others may judge.

3. Lastly, judge how he fleeceth the Country, and inriches himselfe, by considering the vast summe he takes of every towne, he demands but 20.s. a town,&doth sometimes ride 20. miles for that,& hath no more for all his charges thither and back again (& it may be stayes a weeke there) and finde there 3.or 4. witches,or if it be but one,cheap enough,and this is the great summe he takes to maintaine his Companie with 3. horses.

Judicet ullus.

THE END.

Privately Printed Opuscula.

ISSUED TO
MEMBERS OF THE SETTE OF ODD VOLUMES.

No. XXV.

SCOTTISH WITCHCRAFT TRIALS.

Scottish Witchcraft Trials.

BY

J. W. BRODIE-INNES,

Master of the Rolls

TO THE SETTE OF ODD VOLUMES.

Read before the Sette at a Meeting held at Limmer's Hotel, on Friday, 7th November, 1890.

IMPRINTED AT

THE CHISWICK PRESS, TOOKS COURT,

CHANCERY LANE, LONDON.

MDCCCXCI.

This Edition is limited to 245 copies, and is imprinted for private circulation only.

No.........

Presented unto

....

by

....

TO BRO. TYLER.

IN grateful recognition of the generosity which rescued from oblivion the following unworthy effort, and by presenting it to the Sette, and incorporating it with so many works of genius and graceful fancy, has conferred upon it an undeserved immortality; and as a small tribute I dedicate this little volume.

J. W. BRODIE-INNES.

SCOTTISH WITCHCRAFT TRIALS.

YOUR ODDSHIP, BRETHREN, AND GUESTS.

IT is confessedly a matter of extreme difficulty to realize fully the thoughts and motives prompting the actions of men of other times than our own. There is an apparently irresistible tendency in every man to arrogate to his own age, and probably to his own country, the pinnacle of culture and progress, and to regard all the wisdom of the past as steps leading up to that grand result, every point of difference as evidence of ignorance happily dissipated by the sun of modern knowledge. We give, perhaps, an undue value to the art and æsthetic qualities of the past, softened as they are by the mists of time; we may give a grudging recognition to certain ethical qualities in the ages of faith; but that all prior ages were inferior to our own in intellect and science, and a prey to prejudice and superstition, seems firmly fixed as an article of faith of the modern thinker.

Peculiarly is this the case in regard to Witchcraft. The average modern writer on the subject seems only doubtful whether the greatest measure of his scornful pity should be bestowed on the poor silly victims of fantastic delusion, or on the grossly superstitious, ignorant, and bigotted judges who tortured and killed unfortunate persons little above the grade of idiots on account of their delusions. Yet among those witches who were by the courts of Scotland proved and declared to be such, we find persons of high education, culture, and refinement, such as Lady Munro of Fowlis, Lady Glamis, and others; and among judges and others concerned in the Scottish Witchcraft prosecutions, and in the seemingly brutal sentences which were often pronounced, we find some of the keenest philosophical intellects and the greatest minds of the time, men whose works and opinions on every other subject are quoted with respect to this day, of whom it is only necessary to mention the name of Sir George Mackenzie. Clearly the ignorance and superstition theory, though abundantly flattering to the vanity of this age, will not account for the Witchcraft Trials. The mind indignantly refuses to conceive even the possibility of thinking or acting in such a manner. Judges or prisoners, as described on these lines, would be monsters with whom human nature can no more enter into sympathy than it can with the joy of the snake swallowing a guinea-pig.

Recognizing, on the other hand, as we should recognize, that the men of two or three centuries ago were very like ourselves, we might reasonably expect to find in ourselves the germs of the same ideas which bore such strange fruit in the past.

Instinctively the mind settles on the now comparatively familiar phenomena of hypnotism as affording a clue to the difficulty; and, indeed, one of the foremost continental authorities, M. Du Prel, says plainly that a knowledge of hypnotism and somnambulism would throw a very clear light on many of the trials for witchcraft in the Middle Ages. Few, I suppose, could now be found who would deny the possibility of some, at all events, of the alleged phenomena, hypnotism; and the broad lines of these phenomena have been made so familiar by articles and letters in the daily papers and in popular magazines, that it will be enough to postulate a few elementary propositions, proofs of which can be found abundantly in all the scientific works on the subject.

1. The hypnotist can induce a sleep, or a trance, or a cataleptic condition, in which the subject is unconscious of all that passes.

2. Though the subject is conscious of surrounding objects, the hypnotist can induce delusions both positive and negative, causing the subject to see objects not actually there, and causing persons and objects actually before him to become invisible to him.

3. Whether these delusions are produced by suggestion, or by the mere exercise of the will

of the hypnotist, or by some magnetic or other emanation from the operator, they can be so produced that the subject shall not know from whence they proceed.

4. The hypnotist can produce post-hypnotic results, inducing the subject to experience a delusion or to perform an action at a given time long after the hypnotic trance has ended, the subject being then in a waking and apparently normal state, but quite unconscious from whence the impulse proceeds. This action may be a crime.

5. Auto-hypnosis is also possible, in which the subject generates the image himself by an act of his own will or imagination.

These, which are common and well-recognized phenomena, have stirred up a large amount of public attention at present, both here and on the continent, especially in view of the strange new possibilities of crime of which a vista is opened; and it is scarcely to be wondered at that from various sources we hear a demand for legislation on the subject, and for the severe punishment of those who employ the power for criminal or reckless ends.

Dr. Richardson in the "Asclepiad" has referred to what he calls the "Epidemic of Hypnotism," and though his theory is in many respects faulty, and fails to account for well-known facts, he nevertheless calls attention to an important phenomenon, viz., the periodic recurrence of a wide-spread popular interest in the subject. This seems to come at well-marked and almost exact periods of 100 years, and to coincide broadly with the closing years of each century. To take then a leap of a century backwards, over a period when little attention was excited (I am not oblivious of course of the intermediate work of Gregory, Elliotson, Esdaille, Braid, and others; but as a fact, valuable as it was, it roused no pronounced popular interest or excitement), we arrive at an era in this respect much like our own.

Mesmer in Paris was carrying on work of a similar kind, and attracting much the same popular interest as Luys and Charcot are doing now in the same city. And Cagliostro, who, by the way, was by no means the criminal charlatan he has been represented to be, was the exponent of the more occult and mystic side of the same class of phenomena. Another leap of a century brings us once more to a wave of popular attention to the subject. The simultaneous appearance of a number of magnetic healers in England, who worked by touching or stroking, and sometimes by passes, of whom Valentine Greatrakes of Affane was, perhaps, the most notable example; and also of an enormous crop of witchcraft trials and persecutions, and an enormous amount of literature on the subject, the ultimate result of which, in Scotland at any rate, was the final repeal some forty years later of the penal laws against witches, or, in other words, the legislation on the subject of hypnotism, which, now the period having come round again, we are once more demanding; for these penal laws were, as I shall show presently, of a character very like what is now asked for, taking into account the difference of manners and of ideas on criminal jurisprudence. Remarkable at this time is Sir George Mackenzie's account of Witchcraft contained in the tenth title of his Criminal Law, he having a very clear philosophic intellect and discernment, both of the influence of spirits both good and evil more powerful than man, and also of the hypnotic phenomena.

"When we consider," he says, "how the Adamant (*i.e.*, Loadstone) raises and transports the iron, and how the soul of man, which is a spirit, can raise and transport the body, and that a man's voice or a musical sound is able to occasion great and extraordinary motions in other men, we may easily conclude that Devils, who are spirits of far more energy, may produce effects surpassing very far our understanding. And yet I do not deny but that the Devil does sometimes persuade the Witches that they are carried to places where they never were, making these impressions on their spirits and acquainting them what was done there, which is done by imprinting images upon their brain, and which images are carried to the exterior senses by the animal spirits, even as we see the air carries the species of colours upon it, though in a very insensible way; and thus we see likewise that the fumes of Wine or Melancholy will represent strange apparitions, and make us think them real."

This, and other passages too long to quote, show that Mackenzie understood the phenomena of hypnotism, and also that he believed, what some now are coming to think, that there are beings more powerful than man who exercise a similar force, but far more strongly.

Mackenzie, who served as one of the Lords Commissioners of Justiciary until the year 1686, was practically acquainted with his subject. He tells us elsewhere that, as Justice Depute, he went to examine some women who had confessed judicially to being witches.

Yet another century back, and we find a most extraordinary crop of witchcraft trials in Scotland, from the very remarkable case of Elizabeth or Bessie Dunlop, with its graphic details of the

"Court of Faerie," in November, 1576, to the trial of Lady Munro, and her son Mr. Hector Munro, of Fowlis, in July, 1590; and Agnes Sampson in the following January, who was consulted by Bothwell among others.

Of course in the interim there were remarkable trials; the confession of Isobel Goudie, in 1661, is one which could not well be spared in the elucidation of the subject, so full is it of suggestion and of graphic detail, though certainly not fit for general reading. Still, all through the earlier part of the seventeenth century, the letters, diaries, and contemporary records show that the *furore* of belief and interest in witchcraft was flagging, just as the interest in mesmerism or hypnotism was flagging in the early part of the nineteenth century.

Still another leap of a century, and we find ourselves in the period prior to the witchcraft trials, viz., the end of the fifteenth century, yet when the seeds were being sown,—the period of the writings of some of the great alchemists and magicians, when much of occult wisdom and knowledge was being brought before the public and attracting great notice, especially from the fact of its being frequently used by unscrupulous persons for criminal objects, and hence arose a demand similar to the demand which is being made now, that this strange power should be restrained by the hand of the law. The current of popular belief and feeling at that time would be most interesting to trace had we the time, but it is foreign to our subject; suffice it to say, that the end of the fifteenth century passed and nothing was done, beyond that we find the Justice Aire or assize court of Jedworth, in 1510, commissioned to inquire "gif yair be Wichecraift or Sossary wsyt in ye realme"; but the first recorded case was not until 1563, when, on the 26th of June, Agnes Mullikine, alias Bessie Boswell, in Dunfermline, was banished and exiled for witchcraft. This was one of the mildest sentences, perhaps, ever pronounced, but the solitary statute on the matter, which appears among the Scottish Acts, only bears date three weeks before, and was perchance not promulgated at the time. This provides that "na person, of quhat sum ever Estate or condition they be of, take upon hand in onie time hereafter to vse onie manner of Witch craftes, Sorcerie or Necromancie nor giue themselves furth to have onie sik craft or knowledge theirof, theirthrow abusand the people. Nor that na persoun seik onie helpe response or consultation at onie sik users or abusers foresaidis of Witchcraiftes Sorcerie or Necromancie under the pain of death."

This naturally appears at first a very undue penalty for the offence, but if we were to ask any of those good persons who are now quite righteously and properly seeking for some legislative regulation of hypnotism, what the penalty should be for an abuse of that power as compared, for instance, with the theft of a roll of silk from a shop, most would say the former crime was the greater, and should be more severely punished; yet the penalty for the latter was death in the period we speak of.

By 7 Act Stat. David, 2 B. Ch., and cap. 13 b 4 Reg. Mag., one defamed for theft who cannot find caution should be hanged, and Mackenzie concludes that theft is *of its own nature* punishable with death. In fact, 300 years ago the death penalty was thought a generally appropriate one for all persons who seemed likely to be an incurable nuisance to society, though modern sentimentalism has made it seem very strange that such ideas should ever have obtained.

One thing to be specially noted is the concurrence of this statute with other acts of the same period establishing the so-called "Reformed Religion"; the importance of this concurrence will appear as we proceed.

Passing from this date to Nov. 8th, 1576, we come to the trial of Bessie Dunlop, one of the first and perhaps one of the most extraordinary of witchcraft trials in Scotland, or any country. She was indicted on her own confession of using Sorcerie, Incantation, and Invocation of Spirits of the Devil. The circumstances as described seem in brief to have been that she had no art or knowledge herself, but learned all from a man whom she met, whose name was Thom Reid, whom she described as "ane honest elderlie man gray bairded and had ane gray coitt with Lumbard slevis of the auld fassoun a pair of gray brekis and quhyte shankis gartanit aboon the kne, ane blak bonnet on his head closse behind and plain before with silken laisses drawen thro the lippes thereof and ane quhyte wand in his hand." She seems to have been in trouble, and he greets her with "Sancta Maria! Bessie! why makis thow sa grit dule for any worldly thing?"—observe here the Catholic form of salutation. He asks her if she would believe in him, and she says she would believe in any who would do her good. He then promises her great wealth if she would deny her Christianity, and she replies, though she were riven at horse's tails she would never do this. This seems to have been intended as a test, for he did not withdraw his help; but afterwards in his company she saw a gallant band riding past, and he told her these were the "guid wychtis that wonnit in the Court of Elfhame," or the good neighbours that live in the Court of Fairyland. Thom Reid then taught her how to heal, and from the record of cures she seemed to have great power of what is now called faith-healing over both man and beast, power of alleviating the pains of women in childbirth, and the power of the modern thought-reader of finding lost articles. This Thom Reid seems to have told her that he was dead, had been killed at the battle of Pinkye, and that his son Thom Reid the younger was Baron officer to the Laird of Blair. So far, however, she had done nothing but good. She was asked next by the interrogating Court, "Quhat she thoucht of the New Law?" (*i.e.* the Reformed Religion). Answered that she had spoken with Thom about that, but Thom answered "that this new law was nocht gude and that the auld ffayth suld cum hame again but nocht sic as it was befoir." Here seems to lie much of the root of the matter. Bessie seems often to have seen the Court of Fairyland, or Elfhame, as she calls it, riding by to the Middle-earth, which was considered to be their special place. On one occasion she says that "scho had gane afield with hir husband to Leith, for hame bringing of mele and ganging afield to teddir hir naig at Restalrig Loich quhair thair come ane company of Rydaris by that made sic ane dynn as heavin and erd had gane togidder, and incontinent thai raid in to the loich with mony hideous rumbill." Another notable fact in this trial is, that she asked Thom Reid what trouble should come to her for his company, who told her that she should be troubled, but if she could be brought to Glasgow and come into the Bishop's hands, "scho wald be wele trait and sent hame againe." Poor Bessie however did not come to the hands of the Bishop. As usual in such cases, there was a precognition taken before the Privy Council after repeated examinations before the Kirk Session or Presbytery of the Parish, wherein she resided. These inquisitions were held by special commission issued by the Privy Council. In many cases, as for instance, in that of poor Bessie Dunlop, there seems little doubt that the Presbytery set out to find witchcraft in a person who professed the old Catholic faith. The well-known phenomena of hypnotism, faith-healing, and spiritualism, give a perfect clue to all that was charged against Bessie Dunlop, nor is it even necessary to refer to spiritualistic phenomena, if we assume Thom Reid to have been, as most likely he was, a living man and a strong hypnotizer. Not one single instance was brought of the use of her powers for anything but good. But the Kirk Session were bent on "purging the land from Witchcraft." That confessions were often induced by torture is a certain fact, but one which has often puzzled writers on the subject. Of course we can easily see that under torture the unlucky victim would say anything in order merely to be rid of the dregs of her wretched life, but this does not account for the graphic details given by the witches of their experiences, which are of enormous value now in showing the similarity between the witchcraft and sorcery of Scotland, and of other lands and o her races, in the far East and in Africa, many details of which were absolutely unknown to any in Scotland at the time, and could not therefore have been suggested by the tormentors. A far more probable solution seems to lie in the well-known prohibitive power of the hypnotizer of making the subject forget entirely from where the impulse came, and the details of what was seen. The extreme agony of the torture constitutes in itself a re-hypnotization, in which what was formerly *bona fide* forgotten is recalled to memory, constituting what the Germans term Erinnerungs Brücke, or Memory-Bridge, as to which see Moll, "Der Hypnotismus." Among the modern proposals for Legislation on hypnotism, the possibility and desirability of employing the power to detect crimes committed by it, or to induce confession, has been often mooted. Had the Authorities in the sixteenth century possessed a competent knowledge of hypnotism, they would probably never have resorted to the coarse and brutal method of torture. Deprivation of sleep was a common method. Iron collars, or Witches' bridles, are still preserved in many parts of Scotland; a hoop passed over the head, a piece of iron with four prongs was thrust into the mouth, two pointed to the tongue and palate, and two outwards to each cheek. The infernal machine was secured by a padlock, and at the back was a ring by which the prisoner was fastened in a standing position to the wall of the cell, and thus equipped, was night and day regularly waked and watched. One of these instruments now hangs, appropriately enough, in John Knox's house. By such means the Kirk Session rarely failed to procure confessions about the third day. There is little doubt that some such discipline was applied to Bessie Dunlop, who, having been found guilty, was convicted and burnt, or as the sentence ran, "carried to the Castle Hill, and there worried at ane stake and her body burnt to ashes, her whole goods being escheat to the King's use."

Another interesting trial occurs on 28th May, 1588, of Alison Peirsoun. She, under the influence of her cousin William Simpson, whom she speaks of as a great scholar, and doctor of medicine, and who it seems was taken away from his father when but a lad by "ane man of Egypt ane gyant quha had him away to Egypt with him." By the aid of this William Simpson she saw many curious things connected with the Court of Fairyland; *inter alia*, that they maintain their anomalous and intermediate position by paying every year a tribute to the Devil of a tithe of their number, for which cause they are anxious to abstract human children with whom to pay this tribute. The only act positively charged against Alison Pierson, apart from these visions, is the healing of the Bishop of St. Andrews, under the directions of William Simpson. This must have been the celebrated Patrick Adamsoun, and his cure probably is sufficient cause of offence to the Kirk Session.

The next point of special interest is the trial

of Lady Munro of Fowlis, on the 22nd July, 1590. Here whatever practices were used the purpose was undoubtedly criminal, and was largely carried out by poison as well as witchcraft. The purpose of it all was, that by removing Marjory Campbell, the young Lady Balnagown, her brother George Ross of Balnagown might marry Lady Munro, and to do this effectually it was necessary also to destroy her stepson Robert. In this case we get the first authentic account of the use of the waxen images for purposes of enchantment, so familiar now in books of demonologie. The indictment bears, "In the fyrst thow art accusit of making twa pictouris of clay in companie with Christiane Roiss and Marjorie Neyne Mc Allister (alias Loskie Loncart) in the said Christiane Roissis westir chalmer in Canorth, the ane made for the destructioune and consumptioune of the young laird of Fowlis, and the uthir for the young Ladie Balnagown, to the effect that the ane should be put att the Brig end of Fowlis and the uthir att Ardmoir for the destructioune of the saidis young Laird and Lady. And this suld haif bene performit at Alhallowmes in the zeir of God I^{m} V^{c} lxxvij zeiris. Quhilkis twa pictouris being sett on the North syde of the chalmer the said Loskie Loncart tuik twa elf arrows and delyuerit ane to ye Katherene and the uther the said Christiane Roiss Malcumsone held in her awin hand and thow schott twa schottis with the said arrow heid att the said Lady Balnagowne and Loskie Loncart schott thrie schottis at the said young Laird of Fowlis." These details seem to have been supplied from Christiane Roiss' confession. There was also a Katherine Ross implicated, who afterwards married Sir William Sinclair, he who had been the leader of the riot of High School boys when Bailie Macmorran was killed.

In this remarkable case there was undoubtedly some wholesale poisoning, nevertheless Lady Munro and her stepson were acquitted, seemingly by means of very powerful political influence, but the accomplices were condemned and burnt; and notwithstanding the fragmentary and unsatisfactory character of the Reports, probably garbled to allow of Lady Munro's escape, there seems little doubt that her Ladyship was the prime mover in the scheme, and succeeded in hypnotizing her associates for criminal purposes. If we could obtain all the circumstances of this case, it would undoubtedly be of great use in modern proposals for legislation on hypnotism. Whatever else might have been the use of the pictures and ceremonies, they doubtless served to polarize and intensify the evil wills of the circle. Images were also made, as recorded in the evidence, of butter, which is a curious parallel to certain ceremonies recorded by Abbé Huc of the Thibetans.

There are many most interesting trials of this period that must be passed over for lack of space, but some notice must be taken of the case of Dr. Finn, Fian, or Fean, burned in Edinburgh in January, 1591, which presents several features of interest. It seems the Devil preached at North Berwicke Kirk to a number of notorious witches, and Dr. Finn acted as registrar. The means of discovering the doctor's complicity in this work was as follows. A servant girl began to develop a certain healing gift, whereupon, being questioned how it came, she declared she knew nothing, but being put to the torture of the thumbscrew, and her head thrawn with a rope, some words fell from her, leading to the conclusion that she was marked by the Devil, and on search the mark was found on the fore part of her throat.

It may be queried whether this were not somewhat of the nature of the hypnotic zones often referred to by writers on the subject, which being touched or stroked the hypnotic state is revived. Anyhow, this being found she confessed, and in her confession implicated a number of other persons, including Dr. Finn, also called John Cunningham, a schoolmaster at Saltpans in the Lothians. A detailed account of the circumstances of this and some other Witchcraft trials is contained in an extremely rare black letter tract, considered to be unique, called "Newes from Scotland," 1591. Only a few of the most remarkable of the circumstances can be noticed, but the whole story is infinitely curious. The parties seemed to be a group or circle practising hypnotism or spiritualism. Here we find the first notice of the Devil's mark, which students of demonology will remember, and in the pricking or finding of which Matthew Hopkins in England, and John Kincaird of Tranent in Scotland, made a villanous livelihood. Agnes Sampson, the eldest witch of those accused, mentioned that upon Hallowe'en some two hundred witches had put to sea, each one in a riddle or sieve, and went into the same very substantially with flagons of wine, to the Kirk of North Berwick. This recalls Shakespeare's line,

"But in a sieve I'll thither sail,"

and shows his accuracy, for this feat seems peculiar to Scotch witches, at least I do not remember to have see it in any witch stories of England or any other country. This confession, which was made before the King himself, caused him to say "they were all extreame liars," whereupon she told him certain words which had passed in private between the Queen and himself, which he could not but acknowledge to be exact. Dr. Finn, implicated in the same confession, and described as the only man permitted to attend the Devil's readings, was probably the hypnotizer of the circle. He being put to the torture, would not confess, but one of the witches pointed out two pins under his tongue, being the cause whereby he could not confess anything; these being drawn out the charm was lifted and the doctor confessed. It is quite possible here that the doctor, being a somnambulist, had used some form of auto-suggestion and hypnotized himself, inhibiting his own memory of his misdeeds; these appear to have been of the nature of unbridled licentiousness. Wishing on one occasion to use a love charm on a young lady, he endeavoured to procure three hairs wherewith to work his incantation, but her mother being a witch, and fathoming his design, substituted three hairs of a cow, and when the doctor had made his conjuration, the cow came to him at the door of the church, leaping and dancing, and followed him wherever he went. Students of Rabelais will note a similarity here. Having confessed, however, Dr. Finn contrived to escape; being again taken, he utterly denied all his former confession, and the most fearful tortures, graphically described in the Reports, failed to awake memory again, and he was burnt on the Castle Hill.

Agnes Sampsoun, another of the same circle, called the wise wife of Fife, was described by Arnot as "a grave matron-like woman, of rank and comprehension above the vulgar"; and Archbishop Spotswood, speaking of her in much the same terms, says that "she declared she had a familiar spirit who appeared to her in visible form and told her any doubtful matter." She was consulted by Bothwell as to the fate of the

King, and apparently bribed by him to persuade the spirit to compass his death. This the spirit failed to do, and this was apparently the chief cause of her condemnation. She also, however, used charms for her healing, some of which appeared in evidence, and were monkish doggrel rhymes such as are not unknown in nurseries of the present day, one being a rhymed version of the Apostles' Creed, which, doubtless, stank in the nostrils of the saintly Kirk Session. The evidence in her case gives a full and graphic description of a Witches' Sabbath at North Berwick Kirk. There seems great probability that this was really an hypnotic *séance* held by Dr. Finn, wherein, as hinted by Mackenzie, they were persuaded they were carried to places where they never were. The details, however, are very ample of the Devil starting up in the pulpit and calling the roll of their witch nick-names, of the ceremonies of initiation, of their raising bodies in the kirkyard, and of the Devil conjuring wax images and love charms wherewith they should work incantations in future.

She also was burnt on the Castle Hill; and here it may be useful to note, as this burning of witches has been much spoken of as barbarous, etc., that the death penalty was inflicted in various ways in Scotland at this time. Men usually were beheaded—to be hanged was counted very degrading, a fit punishment for a border-thief taken red-handed and executed out of hand, but savouring too much of lynch law for the solemnity of criminal justice. To behead or hang a woman was against the Scottish feeling of the time; women and infirm persons were usually drowned, but women of rank were burnt, as also were women guilty of the higher crimes of treason and murder, to which, on account of its heinousness, witchcraft was added. There was, therefore, no special barbarity in this mode of punishment, which was quite consistent with the criminal ideas of the day.

Barbara Napier, another of the circle, being acquitted by the jurors, an action of wilful error was brought against them on the following 7th of June; they were, however, found not guilty of this.

The most distinguished of the circle was Euphemia or Effiie Makcalzane, the only daughter and heiress of Lord Cliftonhall, a judge of the Court of Session, a man of great learning and attainments, an eminent lawyer, and a great stateman; she married Patrick Moscrop, an advocate of considerable talent, by whom she left three daughters. The charge against her, as against others of the circle, was attempting to compass the King's death by sorcery, images in wax, etc. It is to be noted, however, that she was an ardent Roman Catholic and devoted to the cause of Bothwell, which may throw a side light on her trial. According to Law's "Memorials" Bothwell himself had much traffic with witches, and was esteemed an expert necromancer. She was burnt alive, the severest sentence ever passed by the Court, most of the witches being worried (*i.e.*, strangled) at the stake before being burnt. She met her fate with great firmness, glorying in what she had attempted. The political and religious animosity of the times appears in every line of this trial.

Instances might be multiplied almost *ad infinitum*, and as studies of ceremonial magic 300 years ago, are of very great value. It would, however, be utterly impossible now to enter into more details.

One case only shall be noted, viz., that of Margaret Wallace, the whole pleadings in which are given in full in the 3rd vol. of Pitcairn, and show in a striking way the opinions held by eminent Scotch lawyers on the subject of Witchcraft. In this case it was asserted, though certainly not proved, that she had taken a violent hatred against Cuthbert Grey, and that she threatened his life. According to the evidence Grey had, in fact, persistently abused and threatened her. Howbeit Grey was taken ill, and was lying helpless and unable to move. Margaret Wallace being sent for, "Tuik him by the Schaikill-bane with ane hand and laid her uther hand upone his breast and without any word speaking save only by moving of hir lippes past fra him at that instant: and upon the morn theirefter returning bak again to the s[d] Cuthbert Scho tuik him by the arme and bad him aryse quha at that tyme and fyftene dayis befoir was nocht abill to lift his legis without help yet scho haifing urget him to ryse and taking him by the hand, as said is, broucht him out of his bed and thairefter led him but the house quha immediately thairefter by hir Sorcery and Charmeing practizet by hir, walkit up and down the fluir without help or support of ony and fra that time quickly recovered."

The likeness of this to modern recorded cases of psycho-therapeutics needs no comment.

It remains to see what conclusion can be drawn from all this. It would be absurd to pretend that all mediæval witchcraft was nothing but hypnotism; as absurd, in fact, as to pretend that all the occult phenomena manifested at the present time can be accounted for in the same way. Still, we do see a very striking analogy between these old times and our own.

Then, as now, there came a great wave of phenomena unexplainable by commonly received scientific laws; a probability, indeed an actuality, of some of these phenomena or strange powers being used for criminal purposes, and a demand arose for legislation; this was severe, but considering the severity of all punishments at the time, not out of proportion. But then came the great upheaval of the Reformation, and with it the conviction, probably in many cases honestly entertained, that the devoted adherents of the old faith were bewitched—hypnotized we might say now—and the severity of the law and the obscurity of the crime put a ready weapon into the hands of the triumphant reformers. The publicity of the early witchcraft trials would certainly affect sensitive and imaginative persons, inducing a kind of auto-hypnosis, and the periodic wave I have alluded to would certainly produce a very large number of such sensitives, ready to become somnambulists or clairvoyants with very slight disposing cause. Sensualists, such as probably was Dr. Finn, would seize on the power which probably they would empirically discover. Criminals, political and other, would naturally learn and employ it, and the operation of these causes would increase the popular terror and produce the terrible retributions of panic. These again would operate to spread cases of auto-hypnosis and hysteria, till the wave passed and the symptoms wore themselves out.

Of course this is far from accounting for the whole range of phenomena; indeed, unless we accept the theory of the operation of intelligent powers superior to man, some better and some worse, of an intermediary character, neither wholly good nor wholly evil, it is hard to see how observed phenomena can be accounted for with logical completeness, either to-day or in the sixteenth century. Passing by this, however, there is little doubt that the known results of hypnotism account for much, both then and now, and the unaccounted for residuum is about the same and as perplexing now as it was then.

Furthermore, these old Witchcraft Trials afford a valuable lesson to those who ask for legislation on the subject of hypnotism to-day which they would do well to lay to heart. Not that there should be no such legislation, but that its scope should be most carefully and earnestly considered.

O. V.

A

BIBLIOGRAPHY

OF THE

PRIVATELY PRINTED OPUSCULA

Issued to the Members of the Sette of Odd Volumes.

"Books that can be held in the hand, and carried to the fireside, are the best after all."—*Samuel Johnson.*

"The writings of the wise are the only riches our posterity cannot squander."—*Charles Lamb.*

1. **B. Q.**

A Biographical and Bibliographical Fragment. 22 Pages. Presented on November the 5th, 1880, by His Oddship C. W. H. WYMAN. 1st Edition limited to 25 copies. (Subsequently enlarged to 50 copies.)

2. **Glossographia Anglicana.**

By the late J. TROTTER BROCKETT, F.S.A., London and Newcastle, author of "Glossary of North Country Words," to which is prefixed a Biographical Sketch of the Author by FREDERICK BLOOMER. (pp. 94.) Presented on July the 7th, 1882, by His Oddship BERNARD QUARITCH. Edition limited to 150 copies.

3. **Ye Boke of Ye Odd Volumes.**

from 1878 to 1883. Carefvlly *Compiled* and painsfvlly *Edited* by ye vnworthy Historiographer to ye Sette, *Brother* and *Vice-President* WILLIAM MORT THOMPSON, and produced by ye order and at ye charges of Hys Oddship ye President and Librarian of ye Sette, Bro. BERNARD QUARITCH. (pp. 136.) Presented on April the 13th, 1883, by his Oddship BERNARD QUARITCH.
Edition limited to 150 copies.

4. **Love's Garland;**

Or Posies for Rings, Hand-kerchers, & Gloves, and such pretty Tokens that Lovers send their Loves. London, 1674. A Reprint. And Ye Garland of Ye Odd Volumes. (pp. 102.) Presented on October the 12th, 1883, by Bro. JAMES ROBERTS BROWN.
Edition limited to 250 copies.

5. **Queen Anne Musick.**

A brief Accompt of ye genuine Article, those who performed ye same, and ye Masters in ye facultie. From 1702 to 1714. (pp. 40.) Presented on July the 13th, 1883, by Bro. BURNHAM W. HORNER.
Edition limited to 100 copies.

6. **A Very Odd Dream.**

Related by His Oddship W. M. THOMPSON, President of the Sette of Odd Volumes, at the Freemasons' Tavern, Great Queen Street, on June 1st, 1883. (pp. 26.) Presented on July the 13th, 1883, by His Oddship W. MORT THOMPSON. Edition limited to 250 copies.

7. **Codex Chiromantiae.**

Being a Compleate Manualle of ye Science and Arte of Expoundynge ye Past, ye Presente, ye Future, and ye Charactere, by ye Scrutinie of ye Hande, ye Gestures thereof, and ye Chirographie. *Codicillus I.*—CHIROGNOMY. (pp. 118.) Presented on November the 2nd, 1883, by Bro. ED. HERON-ALLEN. Edition limited to 133 copies.

8. **Intaglio Engraving: Past and Present.**

An Address by Bro. EDWARD RENTON, delivered at the Freemasons' Tavern, Great Queen Street, on December 5th, 1884. (pp. 74.) Presented to the Sette by His Oddship EDWARD F. WYMAN. Edition limited to 200 copies.

9. **The Rights, Duties, Obligations, and Advantages of Hospitality.**

An Address by Bro. CORNELIUS WALFORD, F.I.A., F.S.S., F.R. Hist. Soc., Barrister-at-Law, Master of the Rolls in the Sette of Odd Volumes, delivered at the Freemasons' Tavern, Great Queen Street, on Friday, February 5th, 1885. (pp. 72.) Presented to the Sette by His Oddship EDWARD F. WYMAN. Edition limited to 133 copies.

10. **"Pens, Ink, and Paper:" a Discourse upon Caligraphy.**

The Implements and Practice of Writing, both Ancient and Modern, with Curiosa, and an Appendix of famous English Penmen, by Bro. DANIEL W. KETTLE, F.R.G.S., Cosmographer; delivered at the Freemasons' Tavern, Great Queen Street, on Friday, November 6th, 1885. (pp. 104.) Presented to the Sette on January 8th, 1886, by Bro. DANIEL W. KETTLE. Edition limited to 233 copies.

11. **On Some of the Books for Children of the Last Century.**

With a few Words on the Philanthropic Publisher of St. Paul's Churchyard. A paper read at a Meeting of the Sette of Odd Volumes by Brother CHARLES WELSH, Chapman of the Sette, at the Freemasons' Tavern, on Friday, the 8th day of January, 1886. (pp. 108.) Presented to the Sette by Bro. CHARLES WELSH. Edition limited to 250 copies.

12. **Frost Fairs on the Thames.**

An Address by Bro. EDWARD WALFORD, M.A., Rhymer to the Sette of the Odd Volumes, delivered at Willis's Rooms, on Friday, December 3rd, 1886. (pp. 76.) Presented to the Sette by His Oddship GEORGE CLULOW. Edition limited to 133 copies.

13. **On Coloured Books for Children.**

By Bro. CHARLES WELSH, Chapman to the Sette. Read before the Sette, at Willis's Rooms, on Friday, the 6th May, 1887. With a Catalogue of the Books Exhibited. (pp. 60.) Presented to the Sette by Bro. JAMES ROBERTS BROWN. Edition limited to 255 copies.

14. **A Short Sketch of Liturgical History and Literature.**

Illustrated by Examples Manuscript and Printed. A Paper read at a Meeting of the Sette of Odd Volumes by Bro. BERNARD QUARITCH, Librarian and First President of the Sette, at Willis's Rooms, on Friday, June 10th, 1887. (pp. 86.) Presented to the Sette by Bro BERNARD QUARITCH.

15. **Cornelius Walford: In Memoriam.**

By his Kinsman, EDWARD WALFORD, M.A., Rhymer to the Sette of Odd Volumes. Read before the Sette at Willis's Rooms, on Friday, October 21st, 1887. (pp. 60.) Presented to the Sette by Bro. EDWARD WALFORD, M.A. Edition limited to 255 copies.

16. **The Sweating Sickness.**

By FREDERICK H. GERVIS, M.R.C.S., Apothecary to the Sette of Odd Volumes, delivered at Willis's Rooms, on Friday, November 4th, 1887. (pp. 48.) Presented to the Sette by Bro. FRED. H. GERVIS. Edition limited to 133 copies.

17. **New Year's Day in Japan.**

By Bro. CHARLES HOLME, Pilgrim of the Sette of Odd Volumes. Read before the Sette at Willis's Rooms on Friday, January 6th, 1888. (pp. 46.) Presented to the Sette by Bro. CHARLES HOLME. Edition limited to 133 copies.

18. **Ye Seconde Boke of Ye Odd Volumes,**

from 1883 to 1888. Carefvlly *Compiled* and painsfvlly *Edited* by ye vnworthy Historiographer to ye Sette, Bro. WILLIAM MORT THOMPSON, and produced by ye order and at ye charges of ye Sette. (pp. 157) Edition limited to 115 copies.

19. **Repeats and Plagiarisms in Art, 1888.**

By Bro. JAMES ORROCK, R.I., Connoisseur to the Sette of Odd Volumes. Read before the Sette at Willis's Rooms, St. James's, on Friday, January 4th, 1889. (pp. 33.) Presented to the Sette by Bro. JAMES ORROCK, R.I. Edition limited to 133 copies.

20. How Dreams Come True.

A Dramatic Sketch by Bro. J. TODHUNTER, Bard of the Sette of Odd Volumes. Performed at a Conversazione of the Sette at the Grosvenor Gallery, on Thursday, July 17th, 1890. (pp. 46.) Presented to the Sette by His Oddship Bro. CHARLES HOLME.
Edition limited to 600 copies.

21. The Drama in England during the last Three Centuries.

By Bro. WALTER HAMILTON, F.R.G.S., Parodist to the Sette of Odd Volumes. Read before the Sette at Limmer's Hotel, on Wednesday, January 8th, 1890. (pp. 80.) Presented to the Sette by Bro. WALTER HAMILTON. Edition limited to 201 copies.

22. Gilbert, of Colchester.

By Bro. SILVANUS P. THOMPSON, D.Sc., B.A., Magnetizer to the Sette of Odd Volumes. Read before the Sette at Limmer's Hotel, on Friday, July 4th, 1890. (pp. 63.) Presented to the Sette by Bro. SILVANUS P. THOMPSON. Edition limited to 249 copies.

23. Neglected Frescoes in Northern Italy.

By Bro. DOUGLAS H. GORDON, Remembrancer to the Sette of Odd Volumes. Read before the Sette at Limmer's Hotel, on Friday, December 6th, 1889. (pp. 48.) Presented to the Sette by Bro. DOUGLAS H. GORDON. Edition limited to 133 copies.

24. Recollections of Robert-Houdin.

By Bro. WILLIAM MANNING, Seer to the Sette of Odd Volumes. Delivered at a Meeting of the Sette held at Limmer's Hotel, on Friday, December 7th, 1890. (pp. 81.) Presented to the Sette by Bro. WILLIAM MANNING. Edition limited to 205 copies.

25. Scottish Witchcraft Trials.

By Bro. J. W. BRODIE INNES, Master of the Rolls to the Sette of Odd Volumes. Read before the Sette at a Meeting held at Limmer's Hotel, on Friday, November 7th, 1890. (pp. 66.) Presented to the Sette by Bro. ALDERMAN TYLER. Edition limited to 245 copies.

26. Blue and White China.

By Bro. ALEXANDER T. HOLLINGSWORTH, Artificer to the Sette of Odd Volumes. Delivered at a Meeting of the Sette held at Limmer's Hotel, on Friday, February 6th, 1891. (pp. 70.) Presented to the Sette by Bro. ALEXANDER T. HOLLINGSWORTH.
Edition limited to 245 copies.

27. Reading a Poem.

A Forgotten Sketch by WM. M. THACKERAY. Communicated by Bro. CHAS. PLUMPTRE JOHNSON (Clerke-atte-Lawe to the Sette of Odd Volumes), to the Sette at Limmer's Hotel, on Friday, May 1st, 1891. (pp. xi and 66.) Presented to the Sette by Bro. CHAS. PLUMPTRE JOHNSON. Edition limited to 321 copies.

YEAR-BOKES.

I. The Year-Boke of the Odd Volumes: An Annual Record of the Transactions of the Sette. Eleventh Year, 1888-9.

Written and compiled by Bro. W. MORT THOMPSON, Historiographer to the Sette. Issued November 29th, 1890.

II. The Year-Boke of the Odd Volumes: An Annual Record of the Transactions of the Sette. Twelfth Year, 1889-90.

Written and compiled by Bro. W. MORT THOMPSON, Historiographer to the Sette. Issued April 15th, 1891.
Edition limited to 99 copies.

MISCELLANIES.

1. **Inaugural Address**

of His Oddship, W. M. THOMPSON, Fourth President of the Sette of Odd Volumes, delivered at the Freemasons' Tavern, Great Queen Street, on his taking office on April 13th, &c. (pp. 31.) Printed by order of Ye Sette, and issued on May the 4th, 1883.
Edition limited to 250 copies.

2. **Codex Chiromantiae.**

Appendix A. Dactylomancy, or Finger-ring Magic, Ancient, Mediæval, and Modern. (pp. 34.) Presented on October the 12th, 1883, by Bro. ED. HERON-ALLEN. Edition limited to 133 copies.

3. **A President's Persiflage.**

Spoken by His Oddship W. M. THOMPSON, Fourth President of the Sette of Odd Volumes, at the Freemasons' Tavern, Great Queen Street, at the Fifty-eighth Meeting of the Sette, on December 7th, 1883. (pp. 15.) Edition limited to 250 copies.

4. **Inaugural Address**

of His Oddship EDWARD F. WYMAN, Fifth President of the Sette of Odd Volumes, delivered at the Freemasons' Tavern, Great Queen Street, on his taking office, on April 4th, 1884, &c. (pp. 56.) Presented to the Sette by His Oddship EDWARD F. WYMAN.
Edition limited to 133 copies.

5. **Musical London a Century Ago.**

Compiled from the Raw Material, by Brother BURNHAM W. HORNER, F.R.S.L., F.R. Hist. S., Organist of the Sette of Odd Volumes, delivered at the Freemasons' Tavern, Great Queen Street, on June 6th, 1884. (pp. 32.) Presented to the Sette by His Oddship EDWARD F. WYMAN. Edition limited to 133 copies.

6. **The Unfinished Renaissance;**

Or, Fifty Years of English Art. By Bro. GEORGE C. HAITÉ, Author of "Plant Studies," &c. Delivered at the Freemasons' Tavern, Friday, July 11th, 1884. (pp. 40.) Presented to the Sette by His Oddship EDWARD F. WYMAN. Edition limited to 133 copies.

7. **The Pre-Shakespearian Drama.**

By Bro. FRANK IRESON. Delivered at the Freemasons' Tavern, Friday, January 2nd, 1885. (pp. 34.) Presented to the Sette by His Oddship EDWARD F. WYMAN. Edition limited to 133 copies.

8. **Inaugural Address**

of His Oddship, Brother JAMES ROBERTS BROWN, Sixth President of the Sette of Odd Volumes, delivered at the Freemasons' Tavern, Great Queen Street, on his taking office, on April 17th, 1885, &c. (pp. 56.) Presented to the Sette by His Oddship JAMES ROBERTS BROWN. Edition limited to 133 copies.

9. **Catalogue of Works of Art**

Exhibited at the Freemasons' Tavern, Great Queen Street, on Friday, July 11th, 1884. Lent by Members of the Sette of Odd Volumes. Presented to the Sette by His Oddship EDWARD F. WYMAN. Edition limited to 255 copies.

10. **Catalogue of Manuscripts and Early-Printed Books**

Exhibited and Described by Bro. B. QUARITCH, the Librarian of the Sette of Odd Volumes, at the Freemasons' Tavern, Great Queen Street, June 5th, 1885. Presented to the Sette by His Oddship JAMES ROBERTS BROWN. Edition limited to 255 copies.

11. **Catalogue of Old Organ Music**

Exhibited by Bro. BURNHAM W. HORNER, F.R.S.L., F.R.Hist.S., Organist of the Sette of Odd Volumes, at the Freemasons' Tavern, Great Queen Street, on Friday, February 5th, 1886. Presented to the Sette by His Oddship JAMES ROBERTS BROWN.
Edition limited to 133 copies.

12. **Inaugural Address**

of His Oddship Bro. GEORGE CLULOW, Seventh President of the Sette of Odd Volumes, delivered at the Freemasons' Tavern, Great Queen Street, on his taking office, on April 2nd, 1886, &c. (pp. 64.) Presented to the Sette by His Oddship GEORGE CLULOW.
Edition limited to 133 copies.

13. **A Few Notes about Arabs.**

By Bro. CHARLES HOLME, Pilgrim of the Sette of Odd Volumes. Read at a Meeting of the "Sette" at Willis's Rooms, on Friday, May 7th, 1886. (pp. 46.) Presented to the Sette of Odd Volumes by Bro. CHAS. HOLME. Edition limited to 133 copies.

14. **Account of the Great Learned Societies and Associations, and of the Chief Printing Clubs of Great Britain and Ireland**

Delivered by Bro. BERNARD QUARITCH, Librarian of the Sette of Odd Volumes, at Willis's Rooms on Tuesday, June 8th, 1886. (pp. 66.) Presented to the Sette by His Oddship GEORGE CLULOW.
Edition limited to 255 copies.

15. **Report of a Conversazione**

Given at Willis's Rooms, King Street, St. James's, on Tuesday, June 8th, 1886, by his Oddship Bro. GEORGE CLULOW, *President;* with a summary of an Address on "LEARNED SOCIETIES AND PRINTING CLUBS," then delivered by Bro. BERNARD QUARITCH, *Librarian.* By Bro. W. M. THOMPSON, *Historiographer.* Presented to the Sette by His Oddship GEORGE CLULOW.
Edition limited to 255 copies.

16. **Codex Chiromantiae.**

Appendix B.—A DISCOURSE CONCERNING AUTOGRAPHS AND THEIR SIGNIFICATIONS. Spoken in valediction at Willis's Rooms, on October the 8th, 1886, by Bro. EDWARD HERON-ALLEN. (pp. 45.) Presented to the Sette by His Oddship GEORGE CLULOW.
Edition limited to 133 copies.

17. Inaugural Address

of His Oddship ALFRED J. DAVIES, Eighth President of the Sette of Odd Volumes, delivered at Willis's Rooms, on his taking office on April 4th, 1887. (pp. 64.) Presented to the Sette by His Oddship ALFRED J. DAVIES. Edition limited to 133 copies.

18. Inaugural Address

of His Oddship Bro. T. C. VENABLES, Ninth President of the Sette of Odd Volumes, delivered at Willis's Rooms, on his taking office on April 6th, 1888. (pp. 54.) Presented to the Sette by His Oddship T. C. VENABLES. Edition limited to 133 copies.

19. Ye Papyrus Roll-Scroll of Ye Sette of Odd Volumes.

By Bro. J. BRODIE-INNES, Master of the Rolls to the Sette of Odd Volumes, delivered at Willis's Rooms, May 4th, 1888. (pp. 39.) Presented to the Sette by His Oddship T. C. VENABLES. Edition limited to 133 copies.

20. Inaugural Address

of His Oddship Bro. H. J. GORDON ROSS, Tenth President of the Sette of Odd Volumes, delivered at Willis's Rooms, King Street, St. James's Square, on his taking office, April 5th, 1889. Edition limited to 255 copies.

Ye Sette of Odd Volumes.

1878. BERNARD QUARITCH, *Librarian,* 15, Piccadilly, W. (President, 1878, 1879, and 1882). Original Member.

1878. EDWARD RENTON, *Herald,* 44, South Hill Park, Hampstead, N.W. (Vice-President, 1880; Secretary, 1882). Original Member.

1878. W. MORT THOMPSON, *Historiographer,* 16, Carlyle Square, Chelsea, S.W. (Vice-President, 1882; President, 1883). Original Member.

1878. CHARLES W. H. WYMAN, *Typographer,* 103, King Henry's Road, Primrose Hill, N.W. (Vice-President, 1878 and 1879; President, 1880). Original Member.

1878. EDWARD F. WYMAN, *Treasurer,* 19, Blomfield Road, Maida Vale, W. (Secretary, 1878 and 1879; President, 1884). Original Member.

1878. ALFRED J. DAVIES, *Attorney-General,* Fairlight, Uxbridge Road, Ealing, W. (Vice-President, 1881; Secretary, 1884; President, 1887).

1878. G. R. Tyler, Alderman, *Stationer*, 17, Penywern Road, South Kensington, W. (Vice-President, 1886).

1879. T. C. Venables, *Antiquary*, 9, Marlborough Place, N.W. (President, 1888).

1879. James Roberts Brown, F.R.G.S., *Alchymist*, 44, Tregunter Road, South Kensington, W. (Secretary, 1880; Vice-President, 1883; President, 1885).

1879. George Clulow, *Xylographer*, 51, Belsize Avenue, Hampstead, N.W. (Secretary, 1881; Vice-President, 1884; President, 1886).

1880. Burnham W. Horner, F.R.S.L., *Organist*, 34, Sheen Park, Richmond, S.W. (Vice-President, 1889).

1882. William Murrell, M.D., *Leech*, 38, Weymouth Street, Portland Place, W. (Secretary, 1883; Vice-President, 1885).

1883. Henry George Liley, *Art Director*, Radnor House, Radnor Place, Hyde Park, W.

1883. George Charles Haité, F.L.S., *Art Critic* (**President**), Ormsby Lodge, The Avenue, Bedford Park, W. (Vice-President, 1887).

1883. Edward Heron Allen, *Necromancer*, 2, Ryder Street, St. James's, S.W. (Secretary, 1885).

1884. Wilfrid Ball, R. P. E., *Painter-Etcher* (Vice-President), 39B, Old Bond Street, W. (Master of Ceremonies, 1890).

1884. Daniel W. Kettle, F.R.G.S., *Cosmographer*, Hayes Common, near Beckenham, Kent (Secretary, 1886).

1884. Charles Welsh, *Chapman*, Leytonstone, Essex (Vice-President, 1888).

1885. Edward Walford, M.A., *Rhymer*, 7, Hyde Park Mansions, W.

1886. Charles Holme, F.L.S., *Pilgrim*, The Red House, Bexley Heath, Kent (Secretary, 1887; President, 1890).

1886. Fredk. H. Gervis, M.R.C.S., *Apothecary*, 1, Fellows Road, Haverstock Hill, N.W.

Supplemental Odd Volumes.

1887. JOHN W. BRODIE-INNES, *Master of the Rolls*, Milton House, the Orchard, Bedford Park, W. (Secretary, 1888).

1887. HENRY MOORE, A.R.A., *Ancient Mariner*, Collingham, Maresfield Gardens, N.W.

1887. ALFRED H. LITTLETON, *Troubador*, 22, Hyde Park Square, W.

1887. E. P. LOFTUS BROCK, F.S.A., F.R.I.B.A., *Architect*, 36, Great Russell Street, W.C.

1887. JAMES ORROCK, R.I., *Connoisseur*, 48, Bedford Square, W.C.

1887. W. J. GOODE, *Potter*, Tudor House, Hampstead Heath, N.W.

1888. ALFRED EAST, R.I., *Landscape Painter*, 14, Adamson Road, Belsize Park, N.W.

1888. WALTER HAMILTON, F.R.G.S., F.R.H.S., *Parodist*, Ellarbee, Elms Road, Clapham Common, S.W.

1888. DOUGLAS H. GORDON, F.G.S., *Remembrancer*, 41, Tedworth Square, S.W. (Secretary, 1889).

1888. ALEXANDER T. HOLLINGSWORTH, *Artificer*, 172, Sutherland Avenue, Maida Vale, W. (Vice-President, 1890).

1888. JOHN LANE, *Bibliographer* (Master of Ceremonies), 37, Southwick Street, Hyde Park, W. (Secretary, 1890).

1888. JOHN TODHUNTER, M.D., *Bard*, Orchard Croft, The Orchard, Bedford Park, W.

1889. FRANCIS ELGAR, LL.D., F.R.S.E., *Shipwright*, The Admiralty, Whitehall, S.W.

1889. WILLIAM MANNING, F.R.M.S., *Seer* (Secretary), 21, Redcliffe Gardens, S.W.

1890. SILVANUS P. THOMPSON, D.Sc., M.I.E.E., *Magnetizer*, Morland, Chislett Road, N.W.

1890. CONRAD W. COOKE, M.I.E.E., *Mechanic*, The Lindens, Larkhall Rise, S.W.

1890. E. ONSLOW FORD, A.R.A., *Sculptor*, 62, Acacia Road, N.W.

1891. CHARLES PLUMPTRE JOHNSON, *Clerke atte Lawe* (**Auditor**), 23, Cork Street, W.

1891. FREDERIC VILLIERS, *War Correspondent*, Primrose Hill Studios, N.W.

CHISWICK PRESS:—C. WHITTINGHAM AND CO.
TOOKS COURT, CHANCERY LANE.